MW01488598

THE JESSE TREE

A CHRISTMAS DEVOTIONAL FOR
INDIVIDUALS, COUPLES & FAMILIES

By Chip & Sonya Dodd

The Jesse Tree: A Christmas Devotional for Individuals, Couples, & Families.

Copyright © 2023 by Chip and Sonya Dodd.

All rights reserved. Written permission must be secured from the publisher to use or reproduce any part of this book, except brief quotations in critical reviews or articles.

Scripture quotations marked (NIV) are taken from the New International Version® (NIV)®. Copyright © 1973, 1978, 1984 by International Bible Society. Used by permission of Zondervan Publishing House. All rights reserved.

Scripture quotations marked (NASB) are taken from the New American Standard Bible®, Copyright © 1960, 1971, 1977, 1995, 2020 by The Lockman Foundation. Used by permission. All rights reserved.

Scripture quotations marked (NLT) are taken from the Holy Bible, New Living Translation, copyright ©1996, 2004, 2015 by Tyndale House Foundation. Used by permission of Tyndale House Publishers, Carol Stream, Illinois 60188. All rights reserved.

Scripture quotations marked (NKJV) are taken from the New King James Version®. Copyright © 1982 by Thomas Nelson. Used by permission. All rights reserved.

Cover design: Lauren Jacobs

Text dividers: Doodles by Moonpuff

Chapter images: Flaticon.com

ISBN: 979-8-9854515-5-9

CD Chip Dodd
Resources
chipdodd.com

The Jesse Tree

A Christmas Devotional for Individuals, Couples & Families

General Information

The Jesse Tree is a special Christmas devotional that helps us focus on the upcoming birth of Jesus during the busy month of December. There are 24 devotionals that take us through the Scriptures, beginning with Genesis and ending with the birth of Jesus. The concept of the "Jesse Tree" refers to an image found in the Old Testament:

> *A shoot will come up from the stump of Jesse;*
> *from his roots a Branch will bear fruit.*
> Isaiah 11:1 (NIV)

In this prophetic verse, we learn that Jesus will be born through the line of Jesse, the father of King David. There were many kings who ruled in Israel after King David who did not remain faithful to the One True God, leaving Israel devastated by its enemies. However, this prophetic verse promises that a shoot will come up from the "stump" of what was left of David's kingdom and bear fruit. This Branch or "shoot" is Jesus!

As we prepare our hearts for celebrating the birth of Jesus, we will read a devotional each day and place an ornament that accompanies each story on a Jesse Tree.

The Devotionals

The devotionals in this guide will take you through the Bible, telling the beloved stories of God's remarkable plan to preserve the line out of which would come the Messiah.

Begin reading these daily devotionals on December 1 and continue through December 24. They can be done individually, as a couple, or with family and friends.

Each day has a section called "Extending the Day's Focus." This section offers ideas for deepening and expanding your understanding of the story. It also encourages readers to journal, use research skills, use an atlas, take a fieldtrip, enjoy/create art and music, etc.

We have taken liberty in adding a few details to some of the stories. We did not change any theological or Biblical truths. We used contextual clues, human nature, personal experience, and knowledge of the needs of the human heart to draw conclusions and "fill in the blanks."

chipdodd.com

This devotional guide and printable ornaments are available as a free download at **www.chipdodd.com**.

The Jesse Tree

To enhance the beauty of The Jesse Tree experience, we recommend that you decorate a special "tree" with an ornament each day that relates to the Bible stories in this devotional. This "tree" can be a small store-bought tree, a live tree, a tree made from gathered branches or greenery placed in a vase, a tree drawn on a sheet of poster board, or even a string stretched across a mantle or window that you can attach the ornaments to.

A simple internet search will lead you to a world of ideas for creating a Jesse Tree. You can find many great ideas on Pinterest. Place or arrange this "tree" in a gathering place in your home; it will be a beautiful, visual reminder of the Bible stories you have read and the promises of the coming Savior.

The Ornaments

As part of the daily devotional time, you will hang an ornament on your Jesse Tree. The ornaments will represent some part of the Bible story. Ornaments can be store-bought, handmade, drawn on paper, or you can use the simple, printable ornaments that are available for free download at chipdodd.com. Children will especially enjoy looking at all the ornaments and recalling the Bible stories that accompany them.

There are three sets of free, printable ornaments at **www.chipdodd.com**. There is a simple black and white set and two example sets of do-it-yourself ornaments.

On the internet, you can find many suggestions for making your own ornaments. If you are crafty or have a crafty child/friend, a simple search of "DIY Jesse Tree ornaments" will lead you to a world of ideas for crafting your own unique ornaments.

You can find Jesse Trees and ornaments on Amazon. Etsy is another great place to purchase Jesse Tree items. Just remember that not all Jesse Tree devotionals include the same Bible stories, so if you buy a package of Jesse Tree ornaments, it may not include all the ornaments that go with the stories that we chose for this devotional.

Simple Recommendations

Set aside a special time each day for doing your devotional. If you miss a day, don't quit. Simply skip that day or do two devotionals the next day. Some days you will have more time for your devotional than others; that's okay. We are not striving for perfection; we are reaching for connection.

Choose a comfortable place for doing the daily devotionals. This may be the coffee table in the den, the kitchen table, or just a cozy space. You will want to have your Jesse Tree nearby. You may want to use a box or basket to hold all your Jesse Tree items (this devotional guide, Bibles, ornaments, Bible atlas, Bible story books, paper, colored pencils, crayons, coloring sheets, Play-Doh, etc.). Keeping all the materials in a container will make everything easier.

Suggestions for Families

Make this a joy-filled, peaceful family experience. Even very small children can experience the warm, safe feeling they get when gathered with family. They will associate love and warmth with reading from the Bible.

Because December gets busy quickly, we recommend that you begin planning and preparing for your Jesse Tree experience in November (before the December 1 starting day). Getting a head start is a good idea, especially if you want to make homemade ornaments.

Smaller children who do not have the ability to listen to the whole story may enjoy having a simple activity to do during the devotional time. There are many resources available on the internet. Keep it simple; use items you have around the house. For example: provide drawing paper; print coloring sheets that go with the stories; have Play-Doh available for making story-related items; string macaroni noodles to make a necklace for Queen Esther; etc. Keep it simple and remember not to let the activity become more important than the devotional.

Use your Bible to locate the scripture for each day's devotional. Encourage small children to use their picture Bibles or story books to locate the Bible story for the day. We recommend "The Jesus Storybook Bible" written by Sally Lloyd-Jones for young children. The stories are simple and point to Jesus.

Connect on Social Media

Use these QR codes to take a look at our Facebook and Instagram pages. Both are called "The Jesse Tree: A Christmas Devotional." You will find many simple ideas, pictures, suggestions, and inspiration for making your Jesse Tree Devotional time extra special.

Jesse Tree
Instagram

Jesse Tree
Facebook Page

Capitalizing References to God & Jesus

We primarily used the New International Version (NIV) of the Bible throughout this devotional. While it does not capitalize references to God and Jesus, we capitalize them in the text of this devotional. So, you will see that the text of the devotional has the references to God and Jesus capitalized, but the NIV Bible quotes do not. Hopefully, this won't be confusing.

In Closing

It is our prayer that you, your family, and your friends will stay focused on Jesus this December and be refreshed and renewed by these stories from the Bible that point us to Jesus. We pray that your children will make a heart connection to Scripture and the warm, loving feeling that accompanies it. May God bless you as you make this 24-day journey from creation to the birth of our Savior.

The Jesse Tree

Table of Contents

The Jesse Tree

Ornaments

Day	Ornament
Dec 1	Earth, Animals, Plants, Sun, or Moon
Dec 2	Apple or Serpent
Dec 3	Ark, Rainbow, or Animal/s
Dec 4	Tent, Stars, or Camel
Dec 5	Ram, Altar, Bundle of Sticks, or Stars
Dec 6	Ladder
Dec 7	Colorful Coat or Grain
Dec 8	Baby Moses or Brick
Dec 9	Burning Bush, Staff, or Ten Commandments
Dec 10	Window with Scarlet Cord or Scarlet Cord
Dec 11	Wall or Trumpet (Ram's Horn)
Dec 12	Fleece, Trumpet (Ram's Horn), Clay Jar, Pitcher, or Torch
Dec 13	Wheat
Dec 14	Stump w/Shoot, Sheep, Slingshot, or Crown
Dec 15	Altar, Raven, Fire, or Bucket of Water
Dec 16	Whale or Fish
Dec 17	Crown or Scepter
Dec 18	Lion
Dec 19	Wall or Tools
Dec 20	Praying Hands or Dove
Dec 21	Heart, Angel, or Mary
Dec 22	Saw or Hammer
Dec 23	Mary & Joseph, Donkey, Bethlehem, or Star
Dec 24	Baby Jesus, Manger, Stable, Shepherds, Sheep, Wise Men, Gifts, or Star

December 1
God, the Creator

In the beginning God created the heavens and the earth.
Now the earth was formless and empty, darkness was over the surface of the
deep, and the Spirit of God was hovering over the waters.
Genesis 1:1-2 (NIV)

Then God spoke, "Let there be light" (Genesis 1:3). The light pierced the darkness and day and night began. We soon had the first sunrise and the first sunset and the first stars that twinkled all over the night sky. Waters moved and land began to rise. Soft, thick grass sprung up, and beautiful, fruitful trees whispered in the breezes. Flowers trumpeted, fishes frolicked, dolphins danced, hippos harrumphed, giraffes stretched, cheetahs purred, lambs bleated, and donkeys laughed. Large colorful birds and tiny, fast, sparkling birds called out from everywhere their songs into the days and nights. God spoke all of this creation beauty into being. And God saw all that He had created was "good." Even after creating so much "good," God wanted to do one more powerful and beautiful thing (Genesis 1:10).

Then God said, 'Let us make mankind in our image, in our likeness,
so that they may rule over the fish in the sea and the birds in the sky, over the
livestock and all the wild animals, and over all the creatures that move along the
ground.' So God created mankind in his own image, in the image of God he
created them; male and female he created them.
Genesis 1:26-27 (NIV)

So on the sixth day of creation, God made man and woman, Adam and Eve. "God saw all that he had made, and it was very good" (Genesis 1:31). We were the most special of all.

Adam and Eve were the first people of God, and the place they lived was called the Garden of Eden. It was beautiful and lush. It was Adam and Eve's home. They were the caregivers for all that God had made. They were very joyful together. God was always available to His most precious creation.

Dear God, thank You for revealing Yourself in creation. Open my eyes to see the wonder and beauty of it all.

Additional Bible Reading
Genesis 1-2

Ornament
Earth, Animals, Plants, Sun, or Moon

Extending the Day's Focus
Discuss, journal about, or make a list of what you are most thankful for in God's creation … starry skies, distant thunder, glorious sunsets, quiet snowfalls, prickly pinecones, roly-polies, delicate flower petals, etc.

Take a hike, walk along the beach, or stroll around your neighborhood, focusing on the wonder of God's creation. Pay close attention to the small details that surround you. God had us in mind when He created the earth. Notice and be aware of the tiniest of details that He designed in all His creation … the veins in a leaf, the smell of hay, the rhythm of the waves, the velvety feel of moss, the intricate construction of a bird nest, etc.

Listen to the worship song "So Will I" by Hillsong. Let the lyrics fill your heart and mind as you worship the One True God.

Sketch or paint some of the wonders of God's creation … acorns, palm trees, mountains, starfish, strawberries, clouds, etc. We were created in God's image, and He is creative, so we are, too. Regardless of your opinions of your artistic abilities, you can connect your heart, head and hands with paper, pen, crayon, paint, Play-Doh, yarn, or clay. Play your favorite praise music as you worship God through creating your own masterpieces.

Take or plan a trip to The Creation Museum in Petersburg, Kentucky. This museum features exhibits, speakers, special events, a planetarium, a beautiful botanical garden, a special effects theater, educational programs, a zip line, and more. For more information, visit https://creationmuseum.org.

December 2
Sin Enters the Perfect, Peaceful World

God told Adam that he was "free to eat from any tree in the garden; but you must
not eat from the tree of the knowledge of good and evil,
for when you eat from it you will certainly die."
Genesis 2:16-17 (NIV)

In the middle of the Garden of Eden stood the tree of the knowledge of good and evil. God told Adam that he was free to eat of any tree in the garden except this tree.

There was a creature, a serpent that "was more crafty than any of the wild animals the LORD God had made" (Genesis 3:1). The serpent questioned Eve concerning what God had said to Adam about the tree of the knowledge of good and evil. The evil serpent tricked Eve into believing that what God said about the tree was not true. The serpent's questions caused Adam and Eve to doubt God's goodness and His love for them. In their fear and confusion, they did not cry out to God for help; instead, they turned their hearts away from trusting their loving God and turned toward the conniving serpent, believing his lies. So, when Eve looked at the fruit on the forbidden tree and saw that it was good for eating, pleasant to look at, and that it would make her wise, she took some and ate it. Eve gave some of the fruit to Adam and he ate it (Genesis 3:6). Adam and Eve had been tricked into turning their hearts from God and disobeying His command. Sadly, very sadly, their fear had not led them to cry out to God for help, and everything changed.

As a result of their sin, the sky would become gray. The lamb would no longer nestle with the lion, but run from its roar. The hawk would hunt the mouse to eat. Thorns would grow where flowers had once bloomed, the fruit from trees would begin to rot, and the doves that Adam and Eve had held would fly away from them. And death would enter the world.

But God did not go away; nor did He reject His people. He came into the garden to find Adam and Eve, His loved ones, who were hiding. When God asked, "Where are you?" (Genesis 3:9), He knew exactly where they were physically. God wanted Adam to express where his heart was and what was going on in his heart. He wanted Adam to "cry out" to Him with the truth of the condition of his heart.

Thankfully, Adam told God the truth: "I was afraid … so I hid" (Genesis 3:10). When Adam answered God truthfully, they began to talk about what would have to happen next.

Sin had entered the perfect, peaceful world that God had created. Instead of reaching out to God when the serpent lied to them, they hid their hearts from God. They listened to the serpent who fooled them, instead of listening to the God who created them and loved them. This tragic problem would be our problem from that time until now.

God did not stop loving Adam and Eve then, nor will God ever stop loving us. God even sacrificed some of His own creation to clothe Adam and Eve. They would still have to leave this once-beautiful home because of what they had done.

This was a very sad day for everyone, for God, for Adam, and for Eve. It was not a sad day for the wily serpent, though.

God would not let the serpent win, however.

God prepared a way to save His people. Through Adam, sin entered the world, but God had a plan to save us from our sin through another man who would come to earth a long, long time from then. His name is Jesus. Hope did not die the day Eden ended.

Dear God, thank You for making a way for us to reach You. Give me the courage to "cry out" when I am in need.

Additional Bible Reading
Genesis 3

Ornament
Apple or Serpent

Extending the Day's Focus
Discuss or journal about a time when you did something you really regretted, and you were afraid, but didn't cry out to God. Did you try to fix things by yourself? Did you ask anyone for help?

Visit a botanical garden or look at pictures of botanical gardens on your computer. Talk about or imagine how lush and beautiful the Garden of Eden must have been.

Think about or discuss what it must have been like for Adam and Eve to be able to pet grizzly bears and tigers, or even ride on the backs of crocodiles.

When sin entered the world, everything changed. Adam and Eve had to leave the Garden of Eden. They were sad, but God was with them. He would provide a way for them. Make a list of 10 ways God has provided for you and is still providing.

December 3
Noah's Ark, God's Provision

The LORD saw how great the wickedness of the human race had become on the earth, and that every inclination of the thoughts of the human heart was only evil all the time. The LORD regretted that he had made human beings on the earth, and his heart was deeply troubled. So the LORD said, "I will wipe from the face of the earth the human race I have created—and with them the animals, the birds and the creatures that move along the ground—for I regret that I have made them." But Noah found favor in the eyes of the LORD.
Genesis 6:5-8 (NIV)

After leaving the Garden of Eden, Adam and Eve had children. Their children had more children. The earth began to be populated with lots and lots of people. Instead of working together to do what God had asked them to do in the garden, they continued to tear things to pieces. Instead of caring for each other and the earth, they harmed each other terribly, and they did not honor God or His creation. They did great evil in the face of God. They acted like God was not even alive.

God became very sad about His creation, "and his heart was deeply troubled" (Genesis 6:6). He said, "I will wipe from the face of the earth the human race I have created—and with them the animals, the birds and the creatures that move along the ground—for I regret that I have made them" (Genesis 6:7).

All was not lost, though, because there was a man named Noah who was a good man; he "found favor in the eyes of the LORD" (Genesis 6:8). God looked at his heart (I Samuel 16:7), and He found that Noah wanted to do good; Noah believed in God and knew that God was alive and good (Genesis 6:9).

God talked to Noah. God told Noah to build an ark, a gigantic boat. God told him exactly how to build the ark big enough to hold Noah and his family and all the kinds of animals that God had created.

God told Noah that He was going to bring floodwaters on the earth and destroy all life under the heavens,

> But I will establish my covenant with you, and you will enter the ark—you and your sons and your wife and your sons' wives with you. You are to bring into the ark two of all living creatures, male and female, to keep them alive with you.
> Genesis 6:18-19 (NIV)

Noah did what God told him to do.

The very first rain began to fall, and it rained for forty days and forty nights. The floodwaters covered the whole earth, but Noah and his family, and all of the animals that God loved, too, were safe on the boat.

Finally, the rains stopped and the waters receded. Noah sent a dove out a window in the ark. The dove returned with a freshly picked olive leaf in its beak. A celebration was shouted by Noah and his family. Dry land had returned, and they would be able to start to live on the earth again! It was a fresh beginning.

Then God made a beautiful promise to Noah and to us:

> This is the sign of the covenant I am making between me and you and every living creature with you, a covenant for all generations to come: I have set my rainbow in the clouds, and it will be the sign of the covenant between me and the earth. Whenever I bring clouds over the earth and the rainbow appears in the clouds, I will remember my covenant between me and you and all living creatures of every kind. Never again will the waters become a flood to destroy all life.
> Genesis 9:12-15 (NIV)

Every time we see a rainbow in the sky, we can remember God's unending promise to us. Our hope need never end, and God never stops loving us (Isaiah 54:10 and Psalm 86:15).

Dear God, You always provide a way for us. I am so thankful for that. Open my eyes to see the ways You provide for me.

Additional Bible Reading
Genesis 6-9

Ornament
Ark, Rainbow, or Animal/s

Extending the Day's Focus

Think of a time when you felt you really needed a shower or bath ... after working in the yard on a hot summer day, after playing football, after painting your house, or maybe after walking around an amusement park all day. Did you feel better after a nice shower or bath? It's nice to feel clean and fresh. That's how the earth felt after the cleansing of the flood. When we accept Jesus as our Lord and Savior, we are washed clean of all the sin in our life. Jesus paid the price for our sin through the blood He shed on the cross. Pray together or write a prayer of thanksgiving, thanking God for the cleansing that Jesus offers us through His sacrifice.

Using poster board or large piece of butcher paper, draw and color a mural depicting the story of Noah, the flood, and God's provision.

Take or plan a trip to Williamstown, Kentucky to visit The Ark Encounter. This park features a full-size Noah's ark built according to the specifications given in the Bible. You will truly experience what it was like to be on the ark. The Ark Encounter also features a small zoo, exhibits, zip line, special events, presentations, and more. For more information, visit https://arkencounter.com.

Invite a friend, take the whole family, or go solo to a nearby zoo. Take time to marvel over all the different kinds of animals, insects, reptiles, fish, and habitats you see. What would it have been like for Noah to live on the ark with all the animals and tend to them for months? Discuss or journal your thoughts.

December 4
A Promise to Abraham

"I will make you into a great nation, and I will bless you; I will make your name great, and you will be a blessing."
Genesis 12:2 (NIV)

Despite God's love for His people and His promises to them, they continued to distrust and keep their hearts hidden from Him. They did not ask of God, or seek Him, even though He created them to be in relationship with Him. Even so, God appeared to Abraham and promised to make his descendants into a great nation. This nation would eventually be called Israel. Abraham did not know it, but from this nation and from his descendants, Jesus would come into the world, to save us from our sins. But that would still be a long, long time from then.

God told Abraham to move to a new place. In that new place, God would create a new nation, one that would be for God's people. Abraham believed God, and he gave over his heart to God. God blessed Abraham's willingness to trust, and He said to him:

I will make you into a great nation, and I will bless you;
I will make your name great, and you will be a blessing.
Genesis 12:2 (NIV)

Abraham was married to a beautiful woman named Sarah. They had been married for a long time. They had become quite old, and they still had no children. Abraham began to wonder how God could form a great nation from his family if he had no children. He became sad and confused, so he said to God, "You have given me no children" (Genesis 15:3).

God asked Abraham to trust Him. God took Abraham outside his own tent and said to him: "Look up at the sky and count the stars—if indeed you can count them .... So shall your offspring be" (Genesis 15:5). Abraham believed God even though he did not know how God would do this wonderful thing. God loved Abraham's faith. Abraham continued to trust and wait, and he continued to remember the night God showed him all the stars that he could not count.

Dear God, I am thankful that Abraham believed in Your promises. I want to believe as strongly as Abraham did.

Additional Bible Reading
Genesis 12-15

Ornament
Tent, Stars, or Camel

Extending the Day's Focus
Discuss or journal about a time when you made a big promise to someone or when someone made a big promise to you. What was that promise, and was the promise kept? How did it make you feel that the promise was kept or not kept?

Think of a time when you had to wait a long time for something you really wanted. Was it hard to wait for so long? Did you wait in faith, or did you doubt after a time? Share your thoughts with a friend or write about them in your journal.

If it's a clear night, grab a blanket to spread on the ground and do some stargazing. Invest in or borrow a telescope and look at the stars, planets, and the moon. Observe the expanse of the heavens that God created. Learn to identify some of the constellations and planets in the night sky. You can find lots of star gazing apps on the internet to help you.

Psalm 147:4 says, "He determines the number of the stars and calls them each by name." On a clear night, there are about 3,000-5,000 stars visible to the naked eye. If you could see both hemispheres at the same time, it would be about 6,000-10,000 stars. The Milky Way, our galaxy, has been found to have 200,000 million stars. That is mind-boggling! That God has named every star is beyond comprehension. Discuss or journal what this information means to you.

December 5
Abraham, Isaac, &
The LORD Will Provide

*Abraham answered, "God himself will provide the lamb for the burnt offering,
my son." And the two of them went on together.*
Genesis 22:8 (NIV)

More time passed and many things happened, but Abraham and Sarah still had no children of their own. Then a wonderful thing occurred. God told Abraham that even though he thought he was too old, he would have a son, whom he would call Isaac. Then God assured Abraham that Isaac would indeed be the first of his many descendants. Isaac would grow up and live a long life, and he would have children who would bless many, many others. Abraham continued to believe God and trust Him.

Isaac was born, and Abraham and Sarah were struck with wonder and worshipped God for fulfilling His promise to them. Isaac grew and became a treasure to Abraham and Sarah.

Then, in Genesis 22:1, God spoke to Abraham, and called him by name. Abraham answered God saying, "Here I am." That simple, short response was full of meaning. "Here I am" meant all of me, my whole heart, soul, mind, and strength are here to listen to You. My confidence is in You. You keep Your word to a thousand, thousand generations. Abraham remembered the stars and the promises already fulfilled.

After Abraham responded, God told him to do something very scary, something that did not seem to fit with what God had promised. He told Abraham to take Isaac up on a mountain and sacrifice him as an offering. Even though Abraham would do exactly as God said, he also believed God's earlier promises. As Abraham prepared to sacrifice his one and only son, he told the servants that he and Isaac would return (Genesis 22:5). He told Isaac that God would provide the sacrifice.

Before Abraham could fulfill the sacrifice of Isaac, an angel appeared and told Abraham to stop. The angel said, "Do not lay a hand on the boy …. Do not do anything to him. Now I know that you fear God, because you have not withheld from me your son, your only son" (Genesis 22:12). God did provide a substitute for Isaac. Abraham looked up and saw a ram that was tangled in a thicket. He took the ram and offered it as a sacrifice in place of Isaac.

Then God said to Abraham one more time, "because you have done this and have not withheld your son, your only son, I will surely bless you and make your descendants as numerous as the stars in the sky and as the sand on the seashore …. all nations on earth will be blessed, because you have obeyed me" (Genesis 22:16-18).

Abraham called the place where these things occurred, "The LORD Will Provide" (Genesis 22:14). Abraham believed in God's promises and His provision.

Dear God, thank You that Abraham believed in Your promises and trusted You. Thank You for providing a ram in place of Isaac. Strengthen me that I may believe and trust like Abraham.

Additional Reading
Genesis 21-22:18

Ornament
Ram, Altar, Bundle of Sticks, or Stars

Extending the Day's Focus
Would you have responded to God the way Abraham did? Discuss or journal about how you would have responded to God's testing.

Remember a time when you had to make a heavy sacrifice. Did you struggle with letting go? Were there long-lasting consequences? Do you have regrets? What would you have done differently? Journal or share your thoughts.

The love of a parent for a child is most precious. Take some time to look at old photos of your parents and grandparents. Share any special memories with your family or friends. Do you have any mementos, gifts, or letters? Would you be willing to share those? Not everyone has good memories of parents and grandparents. Are you willing to share or journal about the loss you feel about not having those good memories?

A ram is a male sheep. Use the internet to find out more about the rams that lived in ancient Israel. Where did they live? What did they eat? Journal or share your findings.

December 6

Jacob's Ladder & God's Care for Us

"I am with you and will watch over you wherever you go, and I will bring you back to this land. I will not leave you until I have done what I have promised you."
Genesis 28:15 (NIV)

Isaac was the son of Abraham and Sarah. Isaac married Rebekah, and they lived faithfully and were blessed by God. They were not perfect, just like us; they needed God and cried out to Him. God loved Isaac and Rebekah very much, and they could experience His blessings the most when they were truthful to God about their struggles and needs.

God loves us so much, and He wants to hear from us, guide us, and bless us with good things. He pursues us to make us better people who can help others and care for His creation. Our part is to be honest with God about our hearts. We can freely need God. He created us to be able to reach out to Him. He wants to be in relationship with us.

Jacob was one of Isaac and Rebekah's sons. He did some things that were dishonest (Genesis 27), yet God continued to pursue Jacob to become a person who was truthful and faithful. God had great blessings to give Jacob, just like He wants to give each of us.

However, because of his dishonesty, Jacob had to leave his family and go far away to his uncle's home in Haran. It was a long journey, and he felt all alone. One night when he was asleep, he had an amazing dream. In the dream, Jacob saw a ladder. The bottom of the ladder rested on the earth and the top of it reached all the way to heaven. Jacob saw angels going up and down the ladder. God was standing at the top of the ladder.

In his dream, God promised Jacob, who was Abraham's grandson, that he would be blessed with the land that was promised to his grandfather and his offspring. All peoples of the earth would be blessed through Jacob and his offspring. God's promise would be fulfilled. God also told him that He would go with Jacob wherever he went and watch over him.

Many years later, Jacob would return home to the land of his ancestors. He would take his sons and all his possessions with him. His twelve sons would later form the twelve tribes of Israel. Through Jacob's son, Judah, God would bring forth His son, Jesus. God promised Jacob that from his descendants the whole world would be blessed, and that promise was fulfilled with the birth of Jesus, the Messiah.

Dear God, I thank You that You are so near to us. Help me to look to You and reach out to You when I am in need.

Additional Bible Reading
Genesis 27–33

Ornament
Ladder

Extending the Day's Focus
Discuss or journal about a time when you were struggling with difficult things going on in your life and you needed God. Did you reach out from your heart for God, or did you use your brain to try to fix things yourself? What happened as a result of your choices? Journal about or share your experiences.

Jacob traveled from Beersheba to his uncle's home in Haran. Locate these places on an Old Testament map. How many miles would he have travelled? About how long would it have taken Jacob to go from Beersheba to Haran?

Share or journal about a dream you once had. How did this dream make you feel? What made you dream something like that?

Make a list of the 12 sons of Jacob who would later become the 12 tribes of Israel. Draw a circle around the name of the son whose line would bring forth Jesus, the Messiah.

A theme we see in the story of Jacob is one of God's power and grace to change and renew people. God certainly changed and renewed Jacob. Write a poem, prayer, or song of thanksgiving, thanking God for the changes and renewal you have experienced in your life through His grace and His power.

December 7
Joseph's Coat & God's Favor

"You intended to harm me, but God intended it for good to accomplish what is now being done, the saving of many lives."
Genesis 50:20 (NIV)

Even when we have faith, believe in the kindness of God, and walk in His ways, we still have to face difficulties and struggles. But because of faith; because of our trust in God's kindness and His promises; and because we can go to Him with our pain, we can endure and succeed in spite of painful difficulties. Joseph was a person who walked in faith, and God blessed him mightily, in the midst of very painful times.

Joseph was the next person after Abraham, Isaac, and Jacob who God chose to help make a way for Jesus. He would have a very painful experience, but God raised him to powerful places. What the evil one intended for his evil purposes, God would turn into good!

Joseph was Jacob's son. Jacob loved him very much. Jacob gave him a beautiful coat of many colors. Joseph's older brothers were envious of the coat. Not only that, but Joseph told his brothers about a dream that he had. In the dream, his brothers, and even his mother and father, were bowing down to him (Genesis 37:3-11).

Joseph didn't understand the dream, but when he told his brothers about the dream and how he would one day be more powerful than them, they became even more jealous. Even though each of the brothers had been given the same promises that Abraham, Isaac, and Jacob had received, they were still hateful to Joseph. They even plotted to kill him. But instead, at the last moment, they sold him into slavery, and Joseph was taken to Egypt. His father's heart was broken.

Even in the midst of terrible sadness and confusion for Joseph, God was making a way for him. God had a plan. And the plan was bigger than anyone could even imagine.

While living as a slave in Egypt, Joseph would be falsely accused of doing something bad and thrown into prison. But God even took care of Joseph in prison: "the LORD was with him; he showed him kindness and granted him favor in the eyes of the prison warden" (Genesis 39:21). When Joseph was finally released from prison, he was successful in everything he did because he did it in the name of the LORD with a heart that trusted in God.

Pharaoh, the Egyptian ruler, had a dream that Joseph interpreted. Joseph predicted that Egypt would have seven years of plenty followed by seven years of famine. Pharaoh believed Joseph's prediction. Egypt did have seven years of plenty followed by seven years of famine just as Joseph had said. Pharaoh asked Joseph to oversee the gathering and storing of all the abundance of food during the seven years of plenty. This role placed Joseph in a position of authority. Pharaoh even put Joseph in authority over all of Egypt.

The famine was widespread and even reached the land where Joseph's family still lived. So his brothers came to Egypt looking for food. Although many years had passed, Joseph still recognized them. However, they did not recognize him until Joseph began to weep and told them who he was. The brothers were very frightened that Joseph would want revenge. Instead, he loved them; he had missed them with all his heart. Joseph told them, "'You intended to harm me, but God intended it for good to accomplish what is now being done, the saving of many lives. So then, don't be afraid. I will provide for you and your children.' And he reassured them and spoke kindly to them" (Genesis 50:20-21). Joseph's brothers returned to their homeland. At Joseph's invitation, Jacob left his home in Canaan (Israel), and moved all his family, along with his livestock and all his possessions, to Egypt so that they could be provided for during the famine. They remained in Egypt for many years.

God used the difficult events in Joseph's life to prepare him for this place of significant authority, which allowed him to provide food for his people, the Hebrews. God would always provide a way for His people. Not only did God's people find provision in Egypt during the famine, but hundreds of years later, another family would find safety there. Mary, Joseph, and young Jesus would escape to Egypt to avoid King Herod's wrath.

Had it not been for God's powerful plan to save Egypt, there may not have been an Egypt for Mary, Joseph, and young Jesus to escape to. God is good, even when we cannot see what He is doing. He does everything for our good.

Dear God, thank You for the life of Joseph and for the way he trusted You and believed in You. Make me more trusting like Joseph.

Additional Reading
Genesis 37-50

Ornament
Colorful Coat or Grain

Extending the Day's Focus

Locate Egypt on a map. Find the Nile River. Examine pictures of the pyramids and the Great Sphynx of Giza. Why were these structures built, and what was their purpose? Discuss or journal about your findings.

Using pencils, crayons, or markers, draw pictures of how you think Joseph's colorful coat looked. Display these pictures near your Jesse Tree.

Learn about the different foods and grains that Joseph would have stored up in preparation for the upcoming famine. How would Joseph go about storing up enough food to feed the people of Egypt for seven years? This undertaking was colossal. Discuss or write about how Joseph could accomplish this immense task.

Look for an Egyptian recipe that you can prepare or enjoy a meal at a nearby Egyptian restaurant.

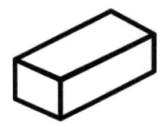

December 8
Moses, Saved for a Purpose

And she named him Moses, and said, "Because I drew him out of the water."
Exodus 2:10 (NASB)

Because Joseph had helped the Egyptians store food to eat during the famine, Joseph's father Jacob, his other 11 sons, and their families moved to Egypt and lived there for a long time. After many years, Jacob passed away. He was buried in his homeland of Canaan, the land that God had promised His people. Today this land is called Israel; it is still the land of the Hebrew or Jewish people and the birthplace of Jesus. As prophesied, Jesus was born in Israel in a little town called Bethlehem.

God would send us Jesus so that we would have a way back to the lives we were created to have from the beginning, even though we still have to live in a broken world where lions growl, snakes have poisonous bites, and hearts get broken. Jesus would be The Way that leads to The Truth about God and to The Life that connects us to God, from our hearts to His heart. Jesus would even say that He is "the way and the truth and the life" (John 14:6). He would also say about Himself that God wants us to "believe in the one he has sent" (John 6:29), the One who is Jesus.

It would still be many years before Jesus, our rescue, would be born. God continued to develop His people and His land to get ready for Jesus' birth. God chose some wonderful people who were very imperfect, and yet very brave and faithful to help make the way for Jesus to come and save us. We can forever be thankful for their faithfulness. One of these brave people was Moses.

Joseph passed away after a long life. A new Pharaoh came to power in Egypt. Joseph meant nothing to the new Pharaoh. He did not honor what Joseph had done to save the Egyptian people from starvation and death. Pharaoh became frightened because the Hebrew population had grown immensely; they were greater and mightier than the Egyptians were. So he decided to enslave the

Israelites. "They made their lives bitter with harsh labor in brick and mortar and with all kinds of work in the fields; in all their harsh labor the Egyptians worked them ruthlessly" (Exodus 1:14).

Pharoah was so fearful and cruel that he even demanded that every baby boy born of a Hebrew be thrown into the Nile River. The Hebrew people were far from their homeland, and were very sad.

One brave woman refused to let her little baby be drowned in the Nile River. When her baby boy was three months old and she could hide him no longer, she took a basket and covered it with tar and pitch to make it waterproof. She put her beautiful baby in the basket and hid him in the reeds along the bank of the Nile River. The waterproof basket became a refuge or ark for the babe. Pharaoh's daughter found the basket in the river and took the baby into her household where he grew up. Even though Moses' mother would always be sad about her loss, she was so grateful that her baby was alive! This baby who lived would be named Moses.

Moses would lead his people out from slavery in Egypt to the land God had promised to give them. While Moses was strong and smart, he was raised in an Egyptian home and did not know the One True God. Moses saw that his enslaved people, the Hebrews, were being treated cruelly by the Egyptians. He wanted to do something about the pain of his people, but he still did not know the One True God. However, God knew Moses. God had a plan for Moses; it was a big plan. God always provides a way for His people, and God was going to use Moses in a very special way.

Dear God, thank You for saving Moses. Thank You for always making a way for us.

Additional Reading
Exodus 1-2:10

Ornament
Baby Moses or Brick

Extending the Day's Focus
Imagine what it would be like to be a Hebrew living in Egypt during the time of enslavement. Discuss or journal about the fears you would have.

Do some research to find out what it was like to live near the Nile River during the time of Moses. What plants and animals lived around the Nile River? What did people eat? What did their homes look like? Discuss or journal your findings.

Baby Moses was laid in a waterproof basket and placed in the Nile River. The basket served as a boat that kept him safe while he floated in the water among the reeds. Noah and his family were kept safe in a boat, too! God made a way for Noah and for Moses. Pray together or write a prayer thanking God for providing safety for Noah and for baby Moses, and for always making a way for His people.

Do an internet search of how to make a paper boat. Using paper that you have available, work together or individually to make small paper boats. Launch them in the sink, tub, or other pool of water. Experiment by covering the hulls of the little boats with different kinds of substances to see if you can make them waterproof (olive oil, tape, wax crayon, etc.).

December 9
The Burning Bush
& the Ten Commandments

"So now, go. I am sending you to Pharaoh
to bring my people the Israelites out of Egypt."
Exodus 3:10 (NIV)

Although Moses was raised to act like an Egyptian, he never lost the experience of knowing in his heart that he was a Hebrew. He saw how badly his people were treated, and he hated this injustice.

Sadly, Moses did not know the God of his people. He did not know how to lead his people or what to do about their distress. "One day, after Moses had grown up, he went out to where his own people were and watched them at their hard labor. He saw an Egyptian beating a Hebrew, one of his own people" (Exodus 2:11). He became furious and took justice into his own hands; he killed the Egyptian soldier and buried him in the sand.

The next day, he saw two Hebrews fighting. Moses asked the one in the wrong why he was hurting his fellow Hebrew. The one in the wrong turned to Moses and said, "Who made you ruler and judge over us? Are you thinking of killing me as you killed the Egyptian?" (Exodus 2:14). Moses was very afraid, but he did not know how to cry out to God.

Pharaoh heard about what Moses had done, and he tried to kill him. Moses was afraid and fled Egypt. He ran to the desert of Midian. When Moses fled, he was also running away from the deepest desire of his heart, to rescue his people from slavery. He did not yet know that God would seek him in the desert and call him to do what he desired to do—liberate God's chosen people, his people.

One day when Moses was tending a flock of sheep on the "far side of the desert," as far away from his past as he could go, something happened that Moses could hardly believe. He saw a burning bush that was not being consumed by its flames. As Moses walked toward the bush, God spoke to him from the burning bush. He told him not to come closer and to take off his sandals because he was standing on holy ground. God identified Himself as the God of Moses' father; the father that Moses never knew. Then God spoke these words to Moses:

> *I am the God of your father, the God of Abraham, the God of Isaac and the God of*
> *Jacob .... I have indeed seen the misery of my people in Egypt.*
> *I have heard them crying out because of their slave drivers, and I am concerned*
> *about their suffering. So I have come down to rescue them from the hand of the*
> *Egyptians and to bring them up out of that land into a good and spacious land,*
> *a land flowing with milk and honey .... So now, go.*
> *I am sending you to Pharaoh to bring my people the Israelites out of Egypt.*
> Exodus 3:6-10 (NIV)

Even though Moses was afraid of what God called him to do, he was full of desire to do God's mission. When Moses spoke his fear to God about not being powerful and his fear that no one would listen to him, God told him, "I will be with you" (Exodus 3:12). Moses would never have to be alone in his struggles again. He would have God to fight for him. God would lead him and His people. God would take care of His people and love them. Moses just needed to follow God.

God used Moses to liberate His people from slavery. As Moses led the Israelites out of Egypt toward the Promised Land, they were faced with many struggles; however, God was always with them. He performed amazing miracles as He provided for them. He parted the Red Sea to make a way for them to escape their enemies. He provided food for them every day. He gave them direction through a pillar of cloud by day and a pillar of fire by night.

Moses learned deep wisdom from God. He was loved and encouraged by God, and he talked with God as a friend to a friend (Exodus 33:11). God would give Moses the greatest, wisest rules for living that the world had ever known. These rules are called the Ten Commandments. God would write these commandments on stone tablets and give them to Moses on Mount Sinai. Moses presented the people with the basic rules of living fully with God and with each other. They said they would obey the commandments so that they would be blessed by their wonderful, good God.

You can read the Ten Commandments in Exodus 20:3-17.

Dear God, I am thankful that Moses, in spite of his fear, still desired to do Your work. Thank You for being with Moses and for strengthening him.

Additional Reading
Exodus 2-20

Ornament
Burning Bush, Staff, or Ten Commandments

Extending the Day's Focus
God spoke to Moses from the burning bush and told him, "I will be with you" (Exodus 3:12). God gave Moses a difficult job, and Moses was fearful that he would not be able to do it. How do you think Moses felt knowing that God would be with him? Have you ever faced a difficult task and felt comfort knowing that God would be with you? Share or journal your thoughts and feelings.

Locate Mount Sinai on an Old Testament map. Where is it located in relation to the Promised Land? What modern day country is Mount Sinai in?

The Bible tells us that God provided manna every day for His people to eat while they were journeying through the wilderness on their way from Egypt to the Promised Land. What was manna? What connection can you draw between God's provision of manna and John 6:48-51? Discuss or journal your thoughts.

Copy the Ten Commandments on paper, poster board, a white board, or your journal. Discuss or journal about the importance and purpose of having laws. Make a list of other areas of life where we have laws.

December 10
Rahab & the Scarlet Cord

For the LORD your God is the supreme God of the heavens
above and the earth below.
Joshua 2:11 (NLT)

God often invites people into His blessings and great purposes who we would not think to invite. Thankfully, our God looks at the heart; He does not just look at appearances. God does not look at a person's expensive clothing, their beauty, their height, or their muscles. God looks for those who will need Him and seek Him with their hearts, as we were created to do from the beginning.

Rahab was an unlikely person for God to choose to help Him make a way for His people. God chose her because of her faithful heart, not her appearance. Rahab was a woman who lived in the city of Jericho. Her home was actually built right into the protective wall that surrounded the city. The people of Jericho did not respect her because of some of the bad choices she had made and the way she chose to live. But Rahab had heard the stories about how God had saved the Israelites from slavery in Egypt, and she knew that God was powerful. God would choose her to help the Israelites conquer Jericho.

There was a man named Joshua who had faith in God. Before Moses died, he chose Joshua to take his place leading the Israelites into the Promised Land. God promised Joshua that He Himself would go with him wherever he went. God said that He would never leave Joshua or forsake him. Joshua learned to be strong and courageous while lingering at the Tent of Meeting where Moses met with God (Deuteronomy 31:7-8 and Exodus 33:11).

As Joshua was leading the Israelites, he sent two spies to search out the city of Jericho whose king was a strong enemy of the Israelites. Their king wanted to stop the Israelites from living in the land that God had promised them. So the spies went to Jericho and came to the house of Rahab, where they found lodging. When the king heard that Israelite spies had entered Rahab's house, he demanded that Rahab send them out so they could be put to death. Instead of sending them out, she hid the men on the roof of her house under some stalks of flax. After the king's men went away, Rahab told the spies that she had heard of their great God who had performed many miracles as He rescued His people from Egyptian slavery. She believed in their God and wanted to follow Him.

Rahab believed that God had given the Israelites the city of Jericho. She asked the spies for a promise that they would protect her and her family when they came to conquer the city since she had treated them with kindness. The men said to her, "we will treat you kindly and faithfully when the LORD gives us the land" (Joshua 2:14). Before she helped them escape out the window of her house, they told her that when they came back to conquer the city, she was to gather her family in her house. They told her to hang a scarlet cord from the same window. When they returned to conquer the city of Jericho, they would see the scarlet cord and spare her and her family.

When Joshua and the Israelites conquered Jericho, Rahab and her family were saved because Joshua's men saw the scarlet cord hanging from her window. She joined the chosen people of God and would ultimately be in the lineage of the One who came to save us all—Jesus! God loves us all and seeks us so that we can have a full life, just like faithful Rahab, who became a friend of God.

Dear God, thank You for the courage of Rahab. Thank You that she is part of the lineage of Jesus.

Additional Bible Reading
Joshua 2 & 6

Ornament
Window with Scarlet Cord or Scarlet Cord

Extending the Day's Focus
Struggling to trust God is part of life. Discuss or journal about some of the struggles you have walked through in your life. What struggles are you facing now? Are you trusting God with your struggles?

Rahab had heard of God's miracles. She knew that God was powerful. She helped Joshua's spies escape out her window. It was from that same window that Rahab hung the scarlet cord. Rahab and all her family were saved when Jericho was destroyed. Rahab was brave and courageous. She wanted to know their God. She was willing to put herself at risk for what she desired. This is called passion. What do you have passion for? Discuss or journal your thoughts.

Rahab had stalks of flax on her roof. What is flax? Why did she have enough flax on her roof for grown men to hide under? What would she have used it for? Journal or discuss your findings.

Tie a scarlet ribbon or string around your wrist. Let it be a reminder that God is always faithful to make a way for His people. The scarlet cord that Rahab hung from her window saved her and her family just like the red blood of Jesus saves us from our sins.

December 11
Joshua, the Trumpets, & the Fall of Jericho

*"Be strong and courageous. Do not be afraid; do not be discouraged, for the LORD
your God will be with you wherever you go."*
Joshua 1:9 (NIV)

God told Joshua to be strong and courageous through faith. God also told Joshua that He would fight for him, and that He would never leave or forsake him. He told Joshua that He would conquer Jericho Himself, but Joshua and his army would need to do exactly as He told them to do. God would show Joshua and the Israelites His power, which went hand in hand with His great love. God said to Joshua:

> *See, I have delivered Jericho into your hands, along with its king and its fighting
> men. March around the city once with all the armed men. Do this for six days.
> Have seven priests carry trumpets of rams' horns in front of the ark.
> On the seventh day, march around the city seven times, with the priests blowing
> the trumpets. When you hear them sound a long blast on the trumpets,
> have the whole army give a loud shout; then the wall of the city will collapse and
> the army will go up, everyone straight in.*
> Joshua 6:2-5 (NIV)

The gates of Jericho were locked tightly because the Israelites had surrounded the city, and no one went in or out. The Israelites did exactly as God had told them. They marched around the city once each day for six days. On the seventh day, what seemed impossible did indeed happen. They marched around the wall of Jericho seven times. The priests blew their ram's horn trumpets. Joshua commanded the people to "Shout! For the LORD has given you the city!" (Joshua 6:16). Joshua believed God and obeyed Him. The wall of Jericho fell and the Israelites conquered the city, just as God had said they would.

God did not forget Rahab, a faithful helper to the Israelites and the only one in Jericho who believed in the One True God. Joshua remembered Rahab and her family. He sent the same two spies to Rahab's house. They saw the scarlet cord hanging from her window! The two men ran inside, and rescued Rahab and all her family. They were given refuge and lived among the people of Israel because of her courage and her belief in the power of the One True God.

A stranger named Rahab received great love and mercy from God. She and her family members were welcomed into the midst of God's chosen people. The story of Rahab ends by saying that Rahab, "lives among the Israelites to this day" (Joshua 6:25). Rahab would even be a part of the lineage out of which Jesus would be born. Our God is gracious to the needy; faithful to the those who depend upon Him; kind to the merciful; and always loving to anyone who will reach for Him.

As Joshua led his men into battle, he remembered that God had told him that He would be with him wherever he went. Joshua could be strong and courageous, knowing that God keeps His promises.

Dear God, I am thankful for Joshua and his leadership of the Israelite people. Even in the aftermath of the battle, he did not forget the promise he made to Rahab.

Additional Bible Reading
Joshua 1-6

Ornament
Wall or Trumpet (Ram's Horn)

Extending the Day's Focus
God used an uncommon battle plan to conquer Jericho. Discuss or journal about His plan for taking the city of Jericho. What was God's strategy? Exactly what did God tell them to do each day? Does this seem like a good battle plan to you?

God gave Joshua an unusual battle plan for conquering the walled city of Jericho. Because no weapons were used, great faith was required. In the end, it was evident who won this battle. Has God ever led you to approach a personal battle in an unusual way? What was the battle you were facing? How did God help you "conquer your Jericho"? How did you feel about God's plan?

Using an Old Testament map, locate the city of Jericho. Search the internet for pictures of how ancient Jericho looked. Imagine what life would be like inside the wall of Jericho. Discuss or journal your thoughts and findings.

Make a list of some of the promises God made to us in the Bible. Do these promises give you comfort? Journal your thoughts.

The Israelites blew trumpets made from ram's horns. Search the internet to find out more about these horns. What is another name for a ram's horn? How were they made? How do they sound? Discuss or journal about your findings.

December 12
Gideon, the Fleece, & the Jars

"The LORD is with you, mighty warrior."
Judges 6:12 (NIV)

The people of God were finally living in the Promised Land, the land that God had promised to faithful Abraham, Isaac, Jacob, Joseph, Moses, and Joshua. Sadly, the people did not follow God's loving commandments; they had begun to put other gods before the One True God. The people did evil in the sight of the One True God. They had turned to other gods. One god they worshipped was named Baal.

Because God's people turned away from the One True God, a cruel tribe of people called the Midianites attacked God's people and overwhelmed them. They swept over their land and carried away their crops of grain and stole their sheep and cattle. The people of God were left with very little food for themselves. They were driven from their villages and farms and had to hide in caves in the mountains. They hid what little food they had where the Midianites could not find it. They were scared and desperate. They wondered If God had abandoned them.

Even though many of them had turned away from God, He remained faithful to them. God sent an angel to a man named Gideon. The angel called out to him and said, "The LORD is with you, mighty warrior" (Judges 6:12). But Gideon doubted the angel. He asked if God had abandoned them since terrible things were happening to them. Then God spoke to Gideon and said, "Go in the strength you have and save Israel out of Midian's hand. Am I not sending you?" (Judges 6:14). Gideon protested again and said, "but how can I save Israel? My clan is the weakest in Manasseh, and I am the least in my family." God patiently calmed Gideon's fear when he said, "I will be with you, and you will strike down all the Midianites ..." (Judges 6:15-16).

Still, Gideon struggled with doubts about trusting God. However, God was patient and loving towards him. As Gideon was gaining faith in what God said He would do, Gideon said to God, "I will place a wool fleece on the threshing floor. If there is dew only on the fleece and all the ground is dry, then I will know that you will save Israel by my hand, as you said." And that is exactly what happened. Gideon rose early the next day. He squeezed the fleece and wrung out the dew—a bowlful of water. Then Gideon said to God, "Do not be angry with me. Let me make just one more request. Allow me one more test with the fleece, but this time make the fleece dry and let the ground be covered with dew. That night God did so. Only the fleece was dry; all the ground was covered with dew" (Judges 6:37-40).

Then Gideon faithfully and courageously put out a call to the men of Israel. He wanted them to join him in fulfilling God's promise to save His people from the hands of the Midianites. God only wanted the most courageous men, so an army of thousands of volunteers shrank to an army of only 300 full-hearted warriors. These 300 men were warriors who would trust God and each other. They would not run away when they became afraid, but instead they would trust in their mighty God who told them to follow Gideon.

On the night that Gideon's 300 men attacked the Midianites, he gave them trumpets, made from ram's horns, and clay jars with torches inside them. After they quietly surrounded the Midianite camp, Gideon then told them:

> *Watch me …. Follow my lead. When I get to the edge of the camp, do exactly as I do. When I and all who are with me blow our trumpets, then from all around the camp blow yours and shout, 'For the LORD and for Gideon.'*
> Judges 7:17-18 (NIV)

Gideon's men did exactly what he told them to do. The Midianites were horrified at the sounds of the trumpets in the pitch dark, the shouts of the men, the fire from the torches glowing, and the crashing sounds of the jars being shattered. The confused Midianites began to attack each other in their horror. They ran into the dark as Gideon's small band of warriors overcame the mighty army of Midianites.

After this great victory, the Israelites wanted Gideon, the mighty warrior, to rule over them. They wanted him to be their king. But Gideon told them, "I will not rule over you, nor will my son rule over you. The LORD will rule over you" (Judges 8:23). Gideon's trust in the Lord brought peace upon the land for years to come. Gideon put no other god before him; he worshipped the One True God, the God who is patient and compassionate, and the God who would bring us King Jesus.

Dear God, I want to be courageous like Gideon. I want to trust You like he did. Strengthen me, Father, to be who You made me to be.

Additional Bible Reading
Judges 6-8

Ornament

Fleece, Trumpet (Ram's Horn), Clay Jar, Pitcher, or Torch

Extending the Day's Focus

When God commanded Gideon to go and save Israel from the hands of the Midianites, Gideon was fearful and lacked courage. He protested and made excuses for why he couldn't do it. Gideon even asked God two different times to confirm that He would indeed use Gideon to defeat the Midianites. Discuss or journal about a time when you lacked courage and confidence and were fearful about doing something that God was asking you to do. What happened? How did you or did you work through your fear and lack of courage and confidence?

Using an Old Testament map, locate Midian. Search the internet and learn about the Midianite people. Were they nomadic or did they build permanent homes? What did they eat? Who did they worship? Were they a peaceful or violent people? Discuss or journal your findings.

God used the lights of torches, the crashing sounds of breaking jars/pitchers, the shouts of the 300 men, and the blasts of trumpets to confuse the Midianite army, allowing Gideon to have victory over them. Can you think of other times in the Bible when God used confusion to fulfill His purposes? Journal or share your findings.

Do an internet search to find out how the people in Bible times made clay pitchers, jars, oil lamps, urns, and other clay items. Use what you have or purchase Play-Doh, modeling clay, polymer clay (Sculpey), or any other type of clay to create pitchers and other vessels. Use them as ornaments or display next to your Jesse Tree.

December 13
Ruth, Boaz, & Loyalty

But Ruth replied, "Don't ask me to leave you and turn back."
Ruth 1:16 (NLT)

The beautiful book of Ruth is a story about loyalty, and how through loyalty our God makes a way, when there seems to be no way. Loyalty is a feeling of devoted attachment and affection. A person who is loyal is someone who displays kindness, trustworthiness, truthfulness, and perseverance. One of the characteristics of God is that He is loyal. God is always loyal to His promises. He is loyal forever, no matter what, to those who seek Him with their whole hearts.

God also loves to bless people who display loyalty to whatever is true, noble, right, pure, lovely, or admirable. Loyal people bless others. The story of Ruth shows us the beauty and the blessing of loyalty. It shows us just how far the blessings of loyalty can reach.

In the days when judges ruled in Israel, a famine came upon the land. So Elimelech took his wife, Naomi, and their two sons and left their home in Bethlehem to go live for a time in the country of Moab. Soon after they left Bethlehem, a very sad and scary thing happened; Naomi's husband died. She was thankful for her two sons, however.

Naomi's sons eventually married Moabite women. These new daughters-in-law were accepted into Naomi's family, even though they were not Israelites. One of them was named Orpah, and the other one was named Ruth. Sadly, after ten years, both of Naomi's sons died, and she and her daughters-in-law were without their husbands.

During those ancient times, a woman who did not have the caring protection of a man was at great risk because she had no one to protect her. Naomi was sad and fearful, as were her sons' wives.

Even though Naomi was distressed, with no husband, sons, or grandchildren, she continued to hope for good and to care for Orpah and Ruth.

Naomi told Orpah and Ruth that she wanted to return to Bethlehem, and that Orpah and Ruth did not have to go with her. They could stay in Moab and maybe marry again and have children.

Naomi loved her two daughters-in-law and said to them, "'Go back to your mothers' homes. And may the LORD reward you for your kindness to your husbands and to me. May the LORD bless you with the security of another marriage.' Then she kissed them good-bye, and they all broke down and wept" (Ruth 1:8-9 NLT).

Orpah chose to remain in Moab. But Ruth clung to Naomi with great care and tenderness in her heart. Ruth spoke the following words of loyalty to Naomi:

> *Don't urge me to leave you or to turn back from you. Where you go I will go, and*
> *where you stay I will stay. Your people will be my people and your God my God.*
> *Where you die I will die, and there I will be buried. May the LORD deal with me, be*
> *it ever so severely, if even death separates you and me.*
> Ruth 1:16-17 (NIV)

Ruth's loyalty to Naomi put her at risk because she was leaving her homeland and going to live with a foreign people who could reject her. Ruth was also going to be with another widow who had no means to be able to take care of herself if the people around her were not generous and merciful. But Ruth loved Naomi. Her heart was connected to Naomi's heart. God would bless Ruth's loyalty.

When Naomi and Ruth arrived in Bethlehem, they needed to find food. Ruth went to the grain fields since it was harvesting time. People who were poor and in need could go to the fields and pick up stalks of grain that workers missed or left behind (this act is called gleaning). Ruth went to the fields in the mornings and worked many hours to gather grain for Naomi and herself.

A man named Boaz owned the field. He was a good man, and he noticed Ruth. He was kin to Naomi's husband. Boaz became a kinsman-redeemer to Naomi and Ruth. A kinsman-redeemer is a male relative who has the privilege of providing and caring for a relative who is in need. Boaz was a caring kinsman-redeemer to Naomi and Ruth.

Boaz was also kin to faithful Rahab, who was a helper to Joshua's spies. While Biblical genealogies don't always include all the names or list them in exact succession, Rahab was Boaz's grandmother, great-grandmother, or more distant ancestor. No matter where Rahab falls in Boaz's family line, the important fact remains that Boaz is a direct descendant of Rahab.

Because Boaz was related to Rahab, he would have heard of the mercy that the Hebrew people extended to Rahab, who was a foreigner. He would have heard about Rahab's fears and struggles as a foreigner in a new land. Boaz was also a loyal man, who loved God. He was a redeemer who cared for those who were in need. He was loyal and did good things. When he saw Ruth, he had compassion for her and was merciful toward her. He even gave her extra measures of grain so that she and Naomi could be secure.

Boaz grew to love Ruth. He admired her loyalty, how hard she worked, and how tender she was to Naomi. They eventually got married and had a son. Naomi, who had endured the grief and fear of losing her husband and two sons, now had a new baby in her life who renewed her heart. The women around Naomi blessed her by saying, "Praise be to the LORD, who this day has not left you without a [kinsman-redeemer]. May he become famous throughout Israel! He will renew your life and sustain you in your old age. For your daughter-in-law, who loves you and who is better to you than seven sons, has given him birth" (Ruth 4:14-15).

Boaz and Ruth named their son Obed. Through Obed, they would be part of the lineage of Jesus. God was making a way to save the world and to heal our hearts. They had no idea that they would be part of bringing our Savior into the world. They were just being faithful to our giving God who has plans for us that are greater than we can possibly imagine.

Dear God, Thank You for Ruth's loyalty and Boaz's mercy. Thank You for making a way for the birth of our Savior, Jesus.

Additional Bible Reading
Ruth 1-4

Ornament
Wheat

Extending the Day's Focus
Discuss or journal about someone in your life who has been faithful in their relationship with you, someone who has been available to listen and to love you in all circumstances. What feelings do you have when you think about this person?

Locate Moab and Bethlehem on an Old Testament map. How far did Naomi and Ruth have to travel? What would the trip have been like for two widowed women? Would they have joined up with a caravan heading in the direction of Bethlehem? Discuss or journal your thoughts and findings.

The words of loyalty that Ruth spoke to Naomi in Ruth 1:16-17, are often used in wedding ceremonies. Discuss or journal about the significance of these verses. Why do you think they are used in weddings?

Discuss or journal about someone who has shown you mercy. What happened that you were in need of their mercy. How did you feel about their offering of mercy?

As widows, Naomi and Ruth were considered outcasts of society. Think about the people who are considered outcasts in your community. Prayerfully consider reaching out to these individuals to offer help. Perhaps you could volunteer with a local ministry that supports people who are in need.

December 14
David, the Shepherd & King

"He is the one who will build a house for my Name,
and I will establish the throne of his kingdom forever."
II Samuel 7:13 (NIV)

Kind Boaz married precious Ruth, and they had a son named Obed, who had a son named Jesse. Jesse had eight sons. His youngest son was named David. He grew up to be King David, the king of Israel. David was the greatest king Israel ever had, until many years later when, through Jesse's line, Jesus would be born. Jesus would be a new kind of king. He would be a king who would rule in our hearts.

But a long time had to pass and a lot more promises had to be fulfilled before King Jesus was born. One of those promises was made to David, a descendant of Ruth.

The story of David is an amazing story. David was a shepherd boy who was anointed king. He was a poet who wrote many of the psalms in the Bible. He was a musician who played the harp and sang songs of praise to God. David was a warrior who fought for justice and righteousness. He was a man who made many mistakes, and yet always came to God for forgiveness. He would be called a man after God's own heart (I Samuel 13:14).

When David was a young man, he was only thought of as the youngest of Jesse's eight sons. All that changed when a prophet named Samuel arrived at his father Jesse's house. God had chosen one of Jesse's sons to be king and had sent Samuel to anoint him. Samuel met each of Jesse's older sons but knew that God had not chosen any of them. Samuel asked Jesse if he had any other sons. "'There is still the youngest,' Jesse answered. 'He is tending the sheep.'" Samuel asked Jesse to send for his youngest son, David. When David arrived, God said to Samuel, "Rise and anoint him; this is the one" (I Samuel 16:11-12). So Samuel anointed David to be the next king of Israel.

David was already brave, even before Samuel anointed him king. He had struck down lions and bears while tending his father's sheep. He had done it by becoming an expert marksman with a sling, out of which he would hurl stones.

After he grew a little older, David did something that would be remembered all over the world forever. He killed a Philistine giant, named Goliath, who threatened to destroy the army of Israel. David told Israel's leaders that he trusted God to fight for Israel, and that he would go to fight Goliath in the name of God (I Samuel 17).

David did just that. While the Israelites and the Philistines watched, young David ran onto the battlefield armed with his faith in God's power, a slingshot, and five smooth stones. By faith, David used his slingshot to bring down Goliath. David proclaimed, "All those gathered here will know that it is not by sword or spear that the LORD saves; for the battle is the LORD's, and he will give all of you into our hands" (I Samuel 17:47).

David eventually became king of Israel. He accomplished much during his reign. David loved God with all his heart. While David was not a perfect king, he worshipped the One True God and never turned to idols as many other kings did. During his life, he demonstrated genuine repentance, and he had a strong passion for spiritual things. There were many kings that reigned after David, but none were as great or as good as David was, until the greatest king the world would ever know came to this earth to save us and redeem us. His name is King Jesus!

There were many kings that ruled in Israel after King David died. Sadly, most of them did not remain faithful to the One True God. As a result, Israel, which was once mighty and powerful, was devastated by its enemies. David's kingdom became a stump of what it once was. But God could use this "stump" of Jesse to bring forth His promise of a Savior and King.

God spoke to His people through the prophet Isaiah, "A shoot will come up from the stump of Jesse; from his roots a Branch will bear fruit" (Isaiah 11:1). Jesse's line had barely survived, but there was life left! And God would protect Jesse's line in order to fulfill His promise of the coming Messiah.

For to us a child is born, to us a son is given, and the government will be on his shoulders. And he will be called Wonderful Counselor, Mighty God, Everlasting Father, Prince of Peace … He will reign on David's throne and over his kingdom … from that time on and forever. The zeal of the LORD Almighty will accomplish this.
Isaiah 9:6-7 (NIV)

Dear God, I'm thankful for the faithful heart of King David. Thank You that he never wavered in his love for You. Strengthen me that I may have a heart more like David's.

Additional Bible Reading
I Samuel 16-II Samuel 24

Ornament
Stump with Shoot, Sheep, Slingshot, or Crown

Extending the Day's Focus
David spent years shepherding his father's sheep. He spent many nights sleeping under God's expansive sky gazing at the twinkling stars and worshipping the Creator. David wrote poems of praise to God. He wrote and sang psalms to God and played his harp in worship to the One True God. Take some time to write a song or poem praising God for who He is and what He has done for you.

Do an internet search of the responsibilities of the shepherds of ancient Israel. Discuss or journal some of the more interesting facts you learn.

Memorize Psalm 23. Imagine David writing this psalm while roaming the hills of his homeland while leading his father's sheep to green pastures.

Goliath was around 9' tall. Measure 9' high on a wall in your home. Put a sticky note at the 9' mark. Leave this note on the wall, NOT to remind you of how big Goliath was, but to remind you that God will fight your battles when you put your trust in Him.

December 15
Elijah Stands Firm for God

"Now I know for sure that you are a man of God,
and that the LORD truly speaks through you."
I Kings 17:24 (NLT)

After King David, there were many kings who were harmful in the way they led the people of God. They refused to worship the One True God who had given them the Promised Land and saved them from many enemies. Sadly, the leaders began to lead the people to worship pagan gods, which God despised.

Because God would never stop loving His people, He kept sending prophets to warn the leaders to stop doing harm to His people and stop rejecting His love for them and the people they led.

It seemed like God's people did not even feel guilty for their behavior. The leaders had lost their sense of conscience, and their hearts had become hard. The people who followed them had also become hard-hearted. But just like a good mom or dad, God would never stop loving His children.

Elijah was one of the great prophets God sent to warn His people. Elijah told God's people to repent, which means to turn away from their harmful actions and hard hearts. He wanted them to return to how God had created them in His image. They were created to follow God; to be caring towards each other; and to care for the lands that God had given them, but they refused again and again.

God told Elijah to go to King Ahab, who was the king at the time. He was evil and had a queen who was even more evil than he was. Her name was Jezebel. She killed many prophets of God. Because she was so evil, the name Jezebel is used to refer to a person who is a cheater, liar, betrayer, and murderer. Ahab and Jezebel worshipped false gods, and they hated the One True God.

Brave Elijah, though, trusted God and loved God. He wanted to do what God wanted him to do to save His people. So he stepped right into the middle of the evil kingdom and told Ahab that the One True God would not tolerate their evil actions anymore. God would stop the rain from falling and the dew from rising for the next years until Elijah told it to rain again. This display of power from God would hopefully get the people to repent.

But instead of repenting, Ahab and Jezebel tried to kill Elijah. God protected him, though. God told Elijah where to hide so that Ahab could not hunt him down and kill him. Elijah's hiding place was by a brook where he had fresh water to drink. God sent ravens to bring Elijah bread and meat in the mornings and the evenings (I Kings 17:6). God will always care for those who will need Him honestly.

God told Elijah to return to Ahab, even at the risk of losing his life. God told him to show the fake prophets of Ahab and Jezebel that the One True God had power and love for His followers that false prophets and false gods did not have.

So Elijah challenged all the false prophets of Ahab and Jezebel to see who was more powerful, the One True God or their false gods. Elijah told Ahab to have all the people of Israel gather at Mount Carmel along with his 850 false prophets. Even though there was no one to physically stand with Elijah, God was with him just like He was with young David when he stepped out to face Goliath. God is near to those who call out to Him.

The false prophets built an altar to their god. They prepared a sacrifice on the altar and cried out to their false god to light the fire and burn the sacrifice. They cried out and danced about and screamed, but nothing happened. Elijah even said to them, "Shout louder .... Perhaps he is deep in thought, or busy, or traveling. Maybe he is sleeping and must be awakened" (I Kings 18:27).

Finally, the false prophets were exhausted; they had failed. Their false god was not the One True God. Then Elijah told the people to come near him. He ordered gallons and gallons of water to be poured on the altar he had prepared. After they poured the water, he told them to pour even more! The water ran down the altar and even filled a deep trench that circled the altar.

Then all the people waited silently as Elijah moved towards the altar. With a loud passionate voice, Elijah prayed to God who is all powerful, "LORD, the God of Abraham, Isaac and Israel, let it be known today that you are God in Israel .... Answer me, LORD, answer me, so these people will know that you, LORD, are God, and that you are turning their hearts back again" (I Kings 18:36-37).

Then the fire of the Lord fell upon the altar, and it "burned up the sacrifice, the wood, the stones and the soil, and also licked up the water in the trench." The people witnessed what happened. They fell on the ground and began to worship, crying out, "'The LORD—he is God! The LORD—he is God!'" (I Kings 18:38-39). All the false prophets who had fooled the people were destroyed. But even though the people cried out and worshipped God, Ahab and Jezebel did not change. They still did not worship God. Instead, they pursued Elijah. They still wanted to destroy him. But God, ever faithful and true, would be with Elijah and save him.

God is powerful to save. We can give thanks to the Lord, "for he is good; his love endures forever" (Psalm 118:1).

Dear God, I praise You for You are the One True God. Thank You for caring for Elijah and for using him to display Your power and might to Your people.

Additional Bible Reading
I Kings 16:29 - I Kings 18

Ornament
Altar, Raven, Fire or Bucket of Water

Extending the Day's Focus
Search the internet to learn about the altars of ancient Israel. What was the purpose of an altar? How were they built? Make a list of other stories in the Bible that include an altar. Share or journal your findings.

Discuss or journal about a time when you felt like you were without family or friends to be with you. You felt alone. What action did you take? Did you slip into self-pity, or did you reach out for someone to be with you? During times when you feel alone, do you call out to God? Do you reach out to friends to be with you? What verses in the Bible bring you comfort when you are feeling alone?

Using a map of Israel, locate Mount Carmel. It is near Haifa, Israel's third largest city. Mount Carmel is actually a mountain ridge located between the Mediterranean Sea and the Jezreel Valley.

When Elijah prayed to God to send fire to burn the sacrifice, God's fire not only burned up the sacrifice, it also burned up the wood, the stones, and the soil, and licked up all the water in the trench around the altar. What a lavish display of power! Our God is NOT the god of "barely making ends meet" or "barely getting by." He is the God of abundance. He is limitless. Discuss or journal about a time when you experienced the lavishness of God. End with a prayer of thanksgiving to God for the unlimited love He has for you.

December 16
Jonah, the Reluctant Prophet

"In my distress I called to the LORD, and he answered me. From deep in the realm of the dead I called for help, and you listened to my cry."
Jonah 2:2 (NIV)

The book of Jonah is an unusual story about an unusual prophet. Unlike other prophets who were called by God to speak His words of truth, Jonah ran from God's call. He did not run from God because God is scary or harsh or mean. He ran from God because God is good and loving towards all people, and merciful to those who will come to Him! Even though Jonah ran, God would pursue Jonah so that he would go and offer God's love to others. God would teach Jonah about His lavish love for him, too.

Jonah was very blessed. He knew that there was only One True God, and he knew that God was a God of love and blessing, mercy and forgiveness. He knew that he was one of the chosen people, one who was favored. He was a Hebrew, kin to Abraham, Isaac, and Jacob. Jonah knew God, and he worshipped Him because he knew that God was the Creator and all powerful. Jonah knew that God was "gracious and compassionate ... slow to anger and abounding in love, a God who relents from sending calamity" (Jonah 4:2). Jonah also knew that if one turned to God, his loving God would pour His love upon the one who turned to Him.

But Jonah did not want to share. He did not want people that he did not like to receive God's blessings. The word of God came to Jonah and told him to go to the large city of Nineveh, a long way from his safe home. Nineveh was a city in Assyria. The king and the people had been thoughtless and selfish. They had even bullied God's people, the Hebrews. God wanted Jonah to tell the people of Nineveh that God was not pleased with their wicked behavior. He wanted these people to repent of their selfish and mean ways and turn to the One who could heal their meanness and make them kind. God desired for the people of Nineveh "to act justly and to love mercy and to walk humbly" with Him (Micah 6:8). But because Jonah did not like these people, who were not like him, he did not want to go and give them God's message. Jonah had forgotten that we cannot earn God's love. He had also forgotten that people who did not know of the One True God could not receive the good news of God unless someone told them. The Ninevites did not know about the love of God.

So rather than obey God, Jonah decided to run away. Jonah ran from his home and away from the people of Nineveh who needed to hear God's message. He went to Joppa and boarded a ship bound for Tarshish, a city that was in the opposite direction of Nineveh. But God pursued him. God sent a great storm upon the sea, and all the sailors became terrified of dying. Finally, Jonah admitted that it was his fault that the seas had become rough. The sailors tried with all their might to row back to shore to save everyone, but they did not have the strength. Jonah asked them to throw him overboard in order to stop the storm. The sailors threw Jonah into the sea, and God instantly stopped the waves and the winds. The sailors were amazed at God's power.

Jonah splashed into the sea, but God sent a great, gigantic fish near the boat to swallow him and save him from drowning. Jonah was in the belly of the fish for three days and nights. While in the fish, Jonah prayed and called out to God for help. Then God told Jonah, again, to go to Nineveh and proclaim His message to the people there. God commanded the fish to go near the shore and spit Jonah out upon the sand. He was very grateful to have been rescued. Jonah obeyed God and headed to the city of Nineveh to proclaim God's message.

Nineveh was a city that was so large it took three days to walk across. When Jonah arrived there, he went straight to the king. He told the king that in forty days the great city would be overthrown. The Ninevites believed God immediately! They declared a fast, "and all of them, from the greatest to the least, put on sackcloth" (Jonah 3:5). The king arose and told all the people, "Let everyone call urgently on God. Let them give up their evil ways and their violence .... God may yet relent and with compassion turn from his fierce anger so that we will not perish" (Jonah 3:8-9). When God saw what they had done and how they turned from their wicked ways, He had compassion, and did not bring destruction upon the people. God was merciful to the people of Nineveh just as He had been merciful to Jonah.

God used Jonah to show His love and mercy to the Assyrian people of Nineveh, but Jonah was not happy about it. Jonah had wanted God to punish the people of Nineveh. Instead, God extended His love beyond the people of Israel. Jonah learned in a very powerful way that all salvation comes from God, and because God is sovereign, He can extend His love and His mercy to anyone.

In the end, Jonah obeyed God, but that didn't mean he had aligned his heart with God's heart. God wanted Jonah's heart to be compassionate toward the people of Nineveh. Sadly, Jonah only performed the act of obedience; he refused to engage his heart.

Dear God, give me a heart that is aligned with Your heart. Strengthen me to be obedient to Your calling for my life.

Additional Bible Reading
Jonah 1-4

Ornament
Whale or Fish

Extending the Day's Focus
Is there something God is asking you to do that you are refusing to do or you are avoiding doing? What is stopping you from being obedient? Discuss or journal your responses.

Imagine what it would be like to be in the belly of a gigantic fish for three days and nights. Make a list of words/phrases that would describe what it would be like. Examples: fishy, salty, stinky, pitch dark, etc.

Have you ever just gotten something done without engaging your heart? Was it homework or job assignment? Perhaps it was mowing the lawn, attending a party or putting the children to bed? Were you just "getting it done" without engaging or attaching your heart? Discuss or journal about what changes or happens to us when we attach our hearts to someone or something. Also discuss or journal about what happens when we do not take the risk of attaching our hearts to others or to what we are doing.

In Colossians 3:23, we read, "Whatever you do, work at it with all your heart, as working for the Lord, not for human masters." Discuss or journal what this verse means to you.

Using a Bible atlas or the internet, find a map of the lands surrounding the Mediterranean Sea during the time of Jonah. Locate the cities of Joppa, Tarshish, and Nineveh. Jonah boarded a ship in Joppa that was bound for Tarshish. Draw a line from Joppa to Tarshish. Draw a line from Joppa to Ninevah, the city that Jonah was supposed to go to. What are the differences between the two journeys? What conclusions can you draw from these findings?

December 17
Courageous Esther Saves Her People

"For if you remain silent at this time, relief and deliverance for the Jews will arise from another place, but you and your father's family will perish. And who knows but that you have come to your royal position for such a time as this?"
Esther 4:14 (NIV)

Very often problems come into our lives that we did not plan, did not cause, and certainly wish we were not faced with. Then, we have to decide if we will move beyond our fear, face the challenge, and take action. Accepting the challenge requires courage, a courage that displays love and reaches beyond our own safety. There are times when you are the only one who can speak and make a difference in times of difficulty. When you could be silent, you are called to speak; when you could be passive, you are called to take action. Esther is a woman of great heart who did just that.

Esther was a Jewish woman living in Persia during the time following the Babylonian destruction of Jerusalem. Many Jews were captured and taken to Babylon to serve as slaves. The book of Ezra tells us that many years later Babylon was captured by King Cyrus of Persia, who gave the Jews the freedom to return to Jerusalem. God moved the hearts of many Jews, and they returned to their homeland. However, many Jews remained in Persia. Some stayed because they were too old to travel or had small children. Others were handicapped, or just did not want to make the long trip. Many were comfortable in Persia or just weren't moved in their hearts to return. Esther's family had remained in Persia.

Esther was orphaned as a child, and her cousin, Mordecai, became her kinsman-redeemer, taking her into his home and caring for her. Years passed and Esther grew into a beautiful woman who was chosen by King Xerxes to be his queen. So Esther became Queen Esther of Persia. Esther was a woman of great character. She displayed her faith in God when she risked her life to save her people. When she could have been silent, she spoke courageously. When she could have been passive, she acted wisely, for such a time as she was needed most.

King Xerxes' ruled over the vast Medo-Persian empire that reached all the way from modern India to modern Ethiopia. He ruled this kingdom from his royal throne in the citadel in the city of Susa.

One day, after Esther became queen, Mordecai uncovered a plot to kill the king. He told Esther about the plot. She reported it to the king and gave credit to Mordecai. The men who plotted to kill the king were punished, and the event was recorded in their history books.

Later, King Xerxes promoted a man named Haman to a place of honor. Haman was manipulative and conniving. He sought power and would do anything to get it. Sadly, the king trusted Haman; he did not know that Haman was betraying him. The king gave Haman a seat of honor greater than all the other nobles. Soon all the royal officials bowed down and paid honor to Haman just as the king had commanded. However, Mordecai refused to bow down to Haman, and this infuriated him. When Haman found out that Mordecai was a Jew, he determined to kill, not just Mordecai, but all the Jews. Haman intentionally misled the king to believe that the Jews were not to be tolerated and must be put to death. Having been convinced of their threat, King Xerxes issued a decree that all Jews throughout the empire were to be put to death.

Everyone was afraid of the king because he was so powerful; he could be ruthless. Anyone who even approached the king without being invited would be put to death unless the king extended his gold scepter to them.

When Mordecai heard about all that had happened and about Haman's plot to have all the Jews exterminated throughout the whole empire, he was devastated. He went to the city gate mourning and wailing. When Esther heard about Mordecai's behavior, she was distressed. She sent a servant to Mordecai to find out what was wrong. Mordecai told Esther's servant everything that had happened. He told the servant to instruct Queen Esther to go to the king and beg for mercy for her people, the Jews. The servant returned to Esther and told her everything.

Queen Esther was afraid. She sent the servant back to Mordecai. She instructed the servant to tell him how dangerous it would be for her to approach the king without first being summoned.

Mordecai responded to Queen Esther by saying, "if you remain silent at this time, relief and deliverance for the Jews will arise from another place, but you and your father's family will perish. And who knows but that you have come to your royal position for such a time as this?" (Esther 4:14). These powerful words to Esther stirred her heart and moved her to step out in passion and faith, taking the risk of losing her own life in order to spare the lives of her people. These words also reflect

Mordecai's faith in God's promise to bring forth the Messiah from among the Jewish people.

Esther sent the servant back to Mordecai to ask him to gather all the Jews in the surrounding area to fast for her for three days. She and her servants would fast, too. After three days, "I will go to the king, even though it is against the law. And if I perish, I perish" (Esther 4:16). During these dark and scary days when it seemed that evil would prevail, God was still sovereign. God was still at work. He had a plan. God always has a plan for His people.

Esther knew what she had to do. Just like David and Elijah, she would stand alone and step out in faith to face her moment of pure and perfect trust in God. She would risk her life for her people. Esther formed a plan. She would approach the king and plead for her people to be spared and expose Haman's wickedness.

Esther dressed in her royal robes and stood in the courts of the palace. When the king saw her, he extended his gold scepter to her! She invited him to a banquet where she pled for him to spare her people, the Jews. The king heard Esther's earnest request and responded favorably.

When King Xerxes realized how he had been tricked by Haman, he was enraged and took action to destroy him. King Xerxes ordered that another decree be written that would overrule the first one, thus sparing the lives of the Jewish people throughout the empire. Esther had indeed acted in courage and faith to save her people.

Esther made a plan, took action, and spoke. She did so at a time when no one else could have. Esther was part of God's plan to protect and preserve the Jewish people in order to fulfill prophecy and bring forth the King of Kings, Jesus.

Dear God, thank You for Esther's courage, her faithfulness, her wisdom, and mostly her willingness to trust You.

Additional Bible Reading
Esther 1-9

Ornament
Crown or Scepter

Extending the Day's Focus
Read Psalm 139:13-16. Esther came to her royal position "for such a time as this." God had a purpose and a plan for Esther's life. He knitted her together in her mother's womb. She was fearfully and wonderfully made. Likewise, God knitted you together in your mother's womb. God also has a purpose and a plan for your life. You, too, are fearfully and wonderfully made. "Your eyes saw my unformed body; all the days ordained for me were written in your book before one of them came to be ...." How do these words affect you? Discuss or journal your feelings and thoughts.

The story of Esther takes place in the Persian city of Susa. Locate ancient Susa on an Old Testament map. Locate Israel on the same map. Queen Esther, Mordecai, and the other Jews of Susa were far away from Israel. In what modern country is Susa located? What is the new name for the ancient city of Susa?

Think about young David as he faced Goliath. Think about Elijah as he stood against 850 false prophets. Think about Queen Esther as she approached the king to plead for her people. What qualities do these three people have? How were they the same? How were they different? Discuss or journal your thoughts.

The Feast of Purim is one of the most fun and joyous holidays celebrated by the Jews. It commemorates the Jews' deliverance from extermination. Search the internet to find out more about this special holiday. Discuss or journal your thoughts and findings.

December 18
Daniel & His Trust of God

"My God sent his angel, and he shut the mouths of the lions. They have not hurt me, because I was found innocent in his sight."
Daniel 6:22 (NIV)

When Daniel, the prophet, wrote the Old Testament book of Daniel, he wanted people to know that our God is sovereign and compassionate forever and ever. He wanted his fellow Jews who were in captivity with him in Babylon, as well as future generations of God's people everywhere, to know three things:

- God is in control over heaven and earth, directing the forces of nature.
- God has the future in His hands, leading all things toward goodness.
- God has care in His heart for all He has created, drawing us towards Him.

Daniel knew that he could trust God completely. He had done so since his youth. And God knew that He could trust Daniel to deliver His message to the people no matter the cost. But just like David, Elijah and Esther, and many other people who trusted in the love of God, Daniel would have to stand alone at times. The good news is that because we are never without our God, we are never truly alone. We can always trust God to be with us, no matter the circumstances.

Just one of the many times that Daniel had to face great difficulties was the day that he was thrown into a den of lions.

Years before this scary thing happened, Daniel and many other gifted young men were captured and taken to Babylon by the Babylonians after they had conquered Jerusalem. These young men were taken from the royal families in Israel. They were "young men without any physical defect, handsome, showing aptitude for every kind of learning, well informed, quick to understand, and qualified to serve in the king's palace" (Daniel 1:4). For three years, they were trained to be in service to the king. They were taught the language and the literature of the Babylonians. They were expected to follow all the Babylonian ways, even down to what they ate and how they prayed.

Daniel and his friends, Hananiah, Mishael, and Azariah, were favored by God because of their trust in Him. God gave them "knowledge and understanding of all kinds of literature and learning. And Daniel could understand visions and dreams of all kinds" (Daniel 1:17). The king would say he "found them ten times better than all the magicians and enchanters in his whole kingdom" (Daniel 1:20).

As Daniel aged and became more experienced and faithful, he continued to rise in power in Babylon. When the next king, Darius, came into power, Daniel was assigned as the head administrator over the whole kingdom. The other administrators and satraps were jealous and tried to find grounds for charges against Daniel so the king would punish him. They could not find anything that he ever did that was dishonest. They could "find no corruption in him, because he was trustworthy and neither corrupt nor negligent" (Daniel 6:4). They tried to harm Daniel because he was favored. They said, "We will never find any basis for charges against this man Daniel unless it has something to do with the law of his God" (Daniel 6:5).

So they designed a devious plan to have Daniel destroyed, even though Daniel was truthful and faithful in all of his ways. He could be trusted to serve the king faithfully because God called him to live faithfully. He was not honest because he was afraid of getting in trouble. Daniel was honest because he loved and trusted the One who created him and loved him. Still, the wicked administrators tried to get him to betray his God with their plan.

They went to the king to trick him. They said the following to the king:

The royal administrators, prefects, satraps, advisers and governors have all agreed that the king should issue an edict and enforce the decree that anyone who prays to any god or human being during the next thirty days, except to you, Your Majesty, shall be thrown into the lions' den.
Daniel 6:7 (NIV)

They knew that Daniel would not pray to anyone or anything other than the God who created him and blessed him. Even though Daniel lived in captivity, very far from the home of his youth, he remained faithful to God. Daniel heard about the decree. Instead of hiding out, Daniel continued to live his faith and remained intimate with God through prayer:

Now when Daniel learned that the decree had been published, he went home to is upstairs room where the windows opened toward Jerusalem. Three times a day he got down on his knees and prayed, giving thanks to his God, just as he had done before. Then these men went as a group and found Daniel praying and asking God for help. So they went to the king and spoke to him about his royal decree: 'Did you not publish a decree that during the next thirty days anyone who prays to any god or human being except to you, Your Majesty, would be thrown into the lions' den?'
Daniel 6:10-12 (NIV)

The king sadly had to support the law that he himself had decreed. The king was very distressed, and just before faithful and favored Daniel was thrown into the lions' den, the king shouted, "May your God, whom you serve continually, rescue you!" (Daniel 6:16). Then, a stone was rolled over the mouth of the lions' den, and the king sealed it so that no escape would be available to Daniel.

The king did not sleep that night. At daybreak, he hurried to the lions' den. He cried out in an anguished voice because he cared for Daniel. He wanted to know if Daniel's God had rescued him. He quickly heard the following words from Daniel:

> *My God sent his angel, and he shut the mouths of the lions.*
> *They have not hurt me, because I was found innocent in his sight.*
> *Nor have I ever done any wrong before you, Your Majesty.*
> Daniel 6:22 (NIV)

The king was overjoyed that God had protected Daniel. When Daniel was taken out of the den of lions, no mark was found on him because he had trusted the One True God.

Then King Darius found out how he had been betrayed by his own people. He punished them by putting them in the lions' den. King Darius then put out a decree to all the people of his empire that they must revere the God of Daniel:

> *For he is the living God and he endures forever; his kingdom will not be*
> *destroyed, his dominion will never end. He rescues and he saves;*
> *he performs signs and wonders in the heavens and on the earth.*
> *He has rescued Daniel from the power of the lions.*
> Daniel 6:26-27 (NIV)

Daniel was willing to stand alone, knowing that as long as he had God with him, he was really never truly alone, even in a lions' den. Daniel lived a perfect picture of how we are to live our lives in faithful service to God. In the midst of captivity and difficulty, Daniel kept his eyes fixed on God and cried out to Him in his time of need regardless of the cost.

Daniel continued to prosper for years and years as he served our God with incorruptible and unwavering devotion.

Dear God, I am amazed by Daniel's conviction to follow You even when it meant he was thrown into the lions' den. Thank You for Your divine protection.

Continued Bible Reading
Daniel 1-6

Ornament
Lion

city, and the temple where they worshipped the One True God.

Nehemiah was the cupbearer to King Artaxerxes. He served the king faithfully, and the king trusted him. Nehemiah had heard from his brother and other men that the wall of Jerusalem was still broken down and that the gates of the city had been burned. His brother told him that the people were in great trouble and disgrace. Nehemiah was stricken with helplessness and homesickness. He "sat down and wept. For some days 'I mourned and fasted and prayed before the God of heaven'" (Nehemiah 1:4). Nehemiah took his pain to God, and he prayed for God to heal Jerusalem.

The next time Nehemiah was in the presence of King Artaxerxes, he could not hide his sadness. The king said to him, "Why does your face look so sad when you are not ill? This can be nothing but sadness of heart" (Nehemiah 2:2). Though Nehemiah was afraid, he told the king about his sorrow. The king asked Nehemiah what he wanted! Nehemiah then asked for the king to release him to return to his homeland and rebuild the wall around the city of Jerusalem. "God had put in my heart to do for Jerusalem" what had not been done (Nehemiah 2:12). Not only did the king release him to go and do God's will, he also sent letters for his safe passage and gave him permission to gather wood from his royal forest.

Nehemiah made the long 900-mile journey to Jerusalem. He called the people together and spoke to their hearts and minds:

> *You see the trouble we are in: Jerusalem lies in ruins, and its gates have been*
> *burned with fire. Come, let us rebuild the wall of Jerusalem,*
> *and we will no longer be in disgrace. I also told them about the gracious hand of*
> *my God on me and what the king had said to me.*
> Nehemiah 2:17-18 (NIV)

The people supported Nehemiah's leadership. They joined God's call upon his heart. They said, "Let us start rebuilding" (Nehemiah 2:18). Even though some people worked against Nehemiah, and some enemies tried to stop the rebuilding, those who joined him "worked with all their heart" (Nehemiah 4:6). With everyone working together and a leader who gave his heart to the mission, the wall was rebuilt in 52 days! Only with God's blessing could the Jews complete this daunting task so quickly. This evidence of God's blessing encouraged the Jews and served as a sign to their enemies that God's blessing was upon them.

Nehemiah became a great administrator and leader for Jerusalem. Nehemiah listened to his heart, and he sought God in his time of great need. God answered his prayer. God took him to the homeland of his people.

Jerusalem is still the homeland of the Jews. Nehemiah played a major role in protecting and preserving this city. As prophesied, Jesus would one day be born in Bethlehem, very near the holy city of Jerusalem. Mary and Joseph could have walked through the gates of this very wall to take baby Jesus to the temple to present Him to the Lord. The story of Nehemiah shows us how much impact just one person can have on a nation.

Dear God, I am thankful for Nehemiah and his ability to lead his people. Thank You that the people responded to Nehemiah's call for help.

Additional Bible Reading
Nehemiah 1-8

Ornament
Wall or Tools

Extending the Day's Focus
The book of Nehemiah comes before the book of Esther in the Old Testament, but historically Esther's story came first. Queen Esther bravely stepped up and saved her people, the Jews, from extermination. If Queen Esther had not spoken up for her people, it is likely that Nehemiah would not have been alive to return to Jerusalem and lead the Jews in rebuilding the protective wall around Jerusalem. King Artaxerxes was kind and generous toward Nehemiah; perhaps it was because he had been influenced by Queen Esther. More than likely, he had heard of her courage and character and her love for her people. Perhaps Queen Esther didn't come to her position as queen only to save her people from Haman's evil plot, but also to influence the king to have compassion for the condition of Jerusalem and to act with generosity toward Nehemiah in his time of need. Discuss or journal your thoughts.

Nehemiah wasn't a priest or a prophet. He was a layman. Nehemiah was the cupbearer to the king. Search the internet or use Bible references to find out the responsibilities of a cupbearer. Share or journal your findings.

Using Legos, clay, Play Doh, blocks, etc. build a replica of the walled city of Jerusalem.

God put in Nehemiah's heart to accomplish this monumental task. The path to fulfilling the task was difficult. But when God calls us to a task, He will make a way. It may not be easy, but He will make a way. Can you think of a time when you felt God was calling you to do something huge for Him? Discuss or journal about this calling and how you responded.

December 20
Zechariah & God's Blessings

But the angel said to him: "Do not be afraid, Zechariah; your prayer has been heard. Your wife Elizabeth will bear you a son, and you are to call him John."
Luke 1:13 (NIV)

God was silent for 400 years between the last of the Old Testament prophets and the birth of Jesus in the New Testament. There were no new Biblical revelations during this time. However, there were significant historical events occurring that would affect the political state of Israel. Many details fell into place in order to prepare for the coming of the Messiah. "But when the fullness of the time had come, God sent forth His Son, born of a woman, born under the law, to redeem those who were under the law, that we might receive the adoption as sons" (Galatians 4:4-5 NKJV).

Many faithful believers continued to remember God's Word and His promises. These believers served God with their whole heart, soul, mind, and strength, and they diligently worked to care for each other. Zechariah and Elizabeth were two of these faithful people. "Both of them were righteous in the sight of God, observing all the Lord's commands and decrees blamelessly" (Luke 1:6). Zechariah was a priest who served in the temple in Jerusalem.

Zechariah and Elizabeth did not have children because Elizabeth was barren. Since they were well along in years, they had given up hope of ever having a child. Then one day, Zechariah was chosen by lot, according to the custom of the priesthood, to be the priest who would go into the temple and burn incense. All the others who had assembled to worship waited outside the temple praying to God. While Zechariah was burning incense, the angel Gabriel appeared to him. God had sent Gabriel to Zechariah to tell him good news.

When Zechariah saw Gabriel, he was very afraid. But the angel comforted him, and told him something wonderful, something the Jewish people had been waiting to hear for thousands of years. Gabriel said:

Do not be afraid, Zechariah; your prayer has been heard.
Your wife Elizabeth will bear you a son, and you are to call him John.
He will be a joy and delight to you, and many will rejoice because of his birth,
for he will be great in the sight of the Lord. He is never to take wine or other
fermented drink, and he will be filled with the Holy Spirit even before he is born.
He will bring back many of the people of Israel to the Lord their God.
And he will go on before the Lord, in the spirit and power of Elijah,
to turn the hearts of the parents to their children and the disobedient
to the wisdom of the righteous—to make ready a people prepared for the Lord.
Luke 1:13-17 (NIV)

When Zechariah heard this wonderful news, he doubted what the angel foretold because he and Elizabeth were quite old. Since he doubted what he had been told, Gabriel said to him, "And now you will be silent and not able to speak until the day this happens, because you did not believe my words, which will come true at their appointed time" (Luke 1:20). Elizabeth became pregnant just as Gabriel said. She was amazed and overwhelmed by joy. Her aged body began to blossom with new life. She was filled with great anticipation. "The Lord has done this for me …. In these days he has shown his favor and taken away my disgrace among the people" (Luke 1:25).

Elizabeth gave birth to a son. When he was eight days old, they named him John, and Zechariah was instantly able to speak again. Immediately he began praising God. Their neighbors were filled with awe, and people throughout the hill country of Judea were talking about this miraculous birth. They were asking, "'What then is this child going to be?' For the Lord's hand was with him" (Luke 1:66).

John would be the cousin of Jesus, the Messiah; he would be called John the Baptist. He would prepare the people for the coming Messiah. John the Baptist preached to the people saying, "Repent, for the kingdom of heaven has come near" (Matthew 3:2). John baptized those people who heard his message proclaimed and sincerely repented of their sins. Eventually, John would baptize Jesus. What an honor and privilege!

These things happened so that the Old Testament prophecies of Isaiah and Malachi would be fulfilled (Isaiah 40:3-5 and Malachi 3:1).

Dear God, Your miracles amaze me! Your ways are perfect, and Your power is unlimited!

Additional Bible Reading
Luke 1 & 3, Matthew 3

Ornament
Praying Hands or Dove

Extending the Day's Focus

Spend some time researching the 400 years of silence. What significant historical events were falling into place that were shaping history and ushering in the fulfilment of Old Testament prophecy? Share or journal your findings.

He and Elizabeth were both from the priestly line of Aaron. Using the internet or Bible reference books, find out what it means to be from the priestly line of Aaron. What were the responsibilities of priests? Share or journal your findings.

In Luke 1, we learn that Zechariah was burning incense in the temple. What is incense? What was the purpose of burning incense in the temple? What was the significance of the altar of incense? Purchase some incense and burn it during tomorrow's Jesse Tree devotional time.

Read Matthew 3:13-17 & Luke 3:21-22. This is the account of John the Baptist baptizing Jesus. What happened when Jesus came up out of the water? What are some other verses in the Bible where we read about a dove? What does a dove symbolize in Scripture? Share or journal your findings.

Search the Old Testament for prophecies about John the Baptist. Find the verses in the New Testament that show the fulfillment of those prophecies. Share or journal your findings.

December 21
Mary, Humble Servant & Mother of Jesus

"I am the Lord's servant," Mary answered. "May your word to me be fulfilled."
Luke 1:38 (NIV)

In the sixth month of Elizabeth's pregnancy, God sent the angel Gabriel to the small town of Nazareth. A young woman named Mary lived there. She was "a virgin pledged to be married to a man named Joseph, a descendant of David" (Luke 1:27). Mary was related to Zechariah's wife, Elizabeth. Perhaps she was Mary's aunt or her cousin.

Gabriel greeted Mary, who was of humble birth, "Greetings, you who are highly favored! The Lord is with you" (Luke 1:28). Mary was distressed, but the angel comforted her. Then Gabriel said:

'Don't be afraid, Mary,' the angel told her, 'for you have found favor with God!
You will conceive and give birth to a son, and you will name him Jesus.
He will be very great and will be called the Son of the Most High. The Lord God will
give him the throne of his ancestor David. And he will reign over Israel forever;
his Kingdom will never end!'
Luke 1:30-33 (NLT)

Sweet Mary wondered how this could be, "since I am a virgin?" (Luke 1:34). The angel told her that the Holy Spirit would cover her with the power of the Most High. "So the holy one to be born will be called the Son of God" (Luke 1:35). The words spoken by Gabriel to Mary would fulfill the great prophecy from Isaiah: "The virgin will conceive and give birth to a son, and will call him Immanuel" (Isaiah 7:14).

Before Gabriel departed, he told Mary that Elizabeth was with child even in her old age, "For nothing will be impossible with God" (Luke 1:37 ESV). Precious Mary said, "I am the Lord's servant …. May your word to me be fulfilled" (Luke 1:38). Gabriel departed. Then the Holy Spirit came upon Mary, and she conceived.

Mary told her parents about Gabriel's visit and his promise that she would be the mother of the coming Messiah. When they heard Mary's words, they were filled with amazement.

It was decided that Mary would go and stay with Elizabeth for a while. Then Mary left her home in Nazareth, her family, and Joseph. She journeyed to a small town in the hill country near Jerusalem where Zechariah and Elizabeth lived. When Mary arrived at their home and greeted Elizabeth, the baby Elizabeth was carrying leapt in her womb, and Elizabeth was filled with the Holy Spirit. She proclaimed to Mary, "Blessed are you among women, and blessed is the child you will bear! But why am I so favored that the mother of my Lord should come to me? As soon as the sound of your greeting reached my ears, the baby in my womb leaped for joy. Blessed is she who has believed that the Lord would fulfill His promises to her!" (Luke 1:42-45).

Then Mary lifted up her voice in praise to God, and she said, "My soul glorifies the Lord and my spirit rejoices in God my Savior" (Luke 1:46-47), for Mary knew that great tidings for all mankind were coming to this world. Mary stayed with Elizabeth for about three months, and then she returned to Nazareth to her family and to her need of Joseph.

The Hebrew people had waited for hundreds and hundreds of years for the fulfillment of the promise of the coming Messiah. They had waited and waited since the days of Eden. Gabriel had spoken the words that the Hebrew people had longed to hear since the days of Noah, and Abraham, Isaac, Jacob, Joseph, and Moses; since the days of Joshua and Rahab, Ruth and Boaz, King David, and Elijah, and Esther; and since the days of Nehemiah.

"A shoot will come up from the stump of Jesse; from his roots a Branch will bear fruit" (Isaiah 11:1). The "shoot" that would come up would be Jesus! Gabriel came to announce the fulfillment of the long-awaited prophecy, that "to us a child is born, to us a son is given ... and he will be called Wonderful Counselor, Mighty God, Everlasting Father, Prince of Peace" (Isaiah 9:6). The Savior was coming to the world, the Messiah, Jesus the Christ!

All the prophecies that spoke of our Savior's birth were about to be fulfilled! We can be thankful for all the faithful servants who deeply longed and desired and hoped for this day to come. They played a vital role in preserving God's people through the ages so that the greatest miracle the world has ever known would be fulfilled, the birth of Jesus, the Messiah!

Dear God, I am so thankful for Mary and her obedience and her willingness to bring the Messiah into the world.

Additional Bible Reading
Matthew 1:18-23 and Luke 1

Ornament
Heart, Angel, or Mary

Extending the Day's Focus
Locate Nazareth and Jerusalem on a map of Israel. Ein Karem is a small village southwest of Jerusalem. Locate Ein Karem. Scholars believe this small village in the Judean hills is where Zechariah and Elizabeth lived and where John the Baptist was born. Trace the route Mary would have likely taken from Nazareth to Ein Karem. She would probably have travelled by donkey. Why do you think Mary made this trip to visit Elizabeth? How long would the trip have taken? What would this trip have been like for a young pregnant girl? Discuss or journal your findings and thoughts.

Growing up in a Jewish family, Mary would have known all about the promised Messiah. Imagine how she felt when the angel told her that she had been chosen by God to be the mother of the long-awaited Messiah. Discuss or journal about how Mary must have felt. Would she be fearful or joyful? Would her parents believe her? Would Joseph believe her? What would her extended family and friends believe about her?

Life in the small town of Nazareth would have been very plain and simple. However, life in the house of a temple priest just outside the holy city of Jerusalem would have been very different. Do some research to find out about life in the house of a temple priest compared to life in Nazareth. Journal or discuss your findings.

Mary stayed with Elizabeth for about three months. Certainly, Mary enjoyed spending this time in Ein Karem so near to the holy city of Jerusalem. Mary learned much from Elizabeth and was encouraged and supported by her. But Mary probably missed her family and Joseph. She was likely homesick for everyone back in Nazareth. Discuss or journal about a time when you were away from family and friends and you were homesick. What or who did you miss the most?

Listen to these two Christmas songs about Mary. Pay close attention to the lyrics. They are powerful. Discuss or journal about your favorite lines.

- "Mary Did You Know?" by Gary Chapman; however, many artists have recorded this beautiful song.
- "Labor of Love" by Andrew Peterson & Jill Phillips (Behold the Lamb of God).

A lovely Christmas tradition is to read the novel *Two from Galilee: The Story of Mary and Joseph* by Marjorie Holmes. This work of fiction tells the love story of Mary and Joseph as it could have happened. You can find it on Amazon and in bookstores.

December 22
Joseph, Husband of Mary & Earthly Father of Jesus

All this took place to fulfill what the Lord had said through the prophet:
"The virgin will conceive and give birth to a son, and they will call him Immanuel"
(which means "God with us").
Matthew 1:22-23 (NIV)

Mary and Joseph were betrothed when the angel Gabriel appeared to Mary. Being betrothed meant that they were legally bound to be married.

When Mary told Joseph she was with child and the circumstances surrounding her pregnancy, he could not grasp that such a miraculous thing had happened to precious Mary. Although Joseph was a good man who was faithful to the law, he struggled to believe it could be true.

Because of their love for each other, they were both troubled and even brokenhearted—Mary, because Joseph struggled to believe her, and Joseph, because he thought Mary might be making up a story about her pregnancy that could not be true. They were also struggling because they were both of humble birth, without social status, and they could hardly grasp that the God of the universe would choose them.

Because Joseph doubted the miracle that had come to Mary, he had in mind to divorce her quietly since he did not want to publicly disgrace her. So an angel of the Lord spoke to him in a dream and said:

*Joseph son of David, do not be afraid to take Mary home as your wife, because
what is conceived in her is from the Holy Spirit.
She will give birth to a son, and you are to give him the name Jesus, because he
will save his people from their sins.*
Matthew 1:20-21 (NIV)

Prophecy was being fulfilled; the Messiah would soon be born: "All this took place to fulfill what the Lord had said through the prophet: 'The virgin will conceive and give birth to a son, and they will call him Immanuel' (which means 'God with us')" (Matthew 1:22-23).

When obedient and faithful Joseph awakened from his dream, he was amazed at the confirmation that his Mary was indeed carrying the Messiah. When precious Mary returned to Nazareth, he took her home to be his wife, as they had originally planned before all these amazing events occurred.

The light and life of the birth of Jesus would soon burst upon the world! Soon, very soon, Jesus, the Messiah, would be born!

Dear God, thank You that Joseph was faithful and honorable. Thank You for his obedience, courage, and willingness to be Jesus' earthly father.

Additional Bible Reading
Matthew 1 and Luke 1

Ornament
Saw or Hammer

Extending the Day's Focus
Joseph was a carpenter. He created and worked with his hands. Most likely he learned how to be a carpenter from his father. Do some research to find out what life would be like for a carpenter in the small town of Nazareth during this time. What kinds of tools would Joseph use? What items would Joseph make/build? Would he travel to neighboring towns to work? Discuss or journal what you learn from your research.

What kinds of trees grew in and around Nazareth? Which woods were good for building? Which woods were better for building a fire? Do you think Joseph would ever have travelled far away to bring back different kinds of wood to work with? Journal or share your findings and thoughts.

God would certainly want Jesus's earthly father to be a good and faithful man. Discuss or journal about the qualities and characteristics that Joseph more than likely possessed that made him God's choice for the man who would raise His one and only Son. How would Joseph's training and experience as a carpenter prepare him for the role of husband to Mary and father to Jesus? Discuss or journal your thoughts.

Imagine what it would be like to be the earthly father of the Son of God. Would you feel extra protective? Would you, at times, feel overwhelmed with the task of raising Jesus, the Son of God? Discuss or journal your thoughts.

If you have tools and wood, build something simple like a birdhouse or a box. Perhaps you could make a simple Christmas ornament or build a nativity stable or a small manger. Young children could use toy tools and pretend to be Joseph and Jesus in their workshop.

December 23
Mary & Joseph Journey to Bethlehem

"But you, Bethlehem Ephrathah, though you are small among the clans of Judah,
out of you will come for me one who will be ruler over Israel, whose origins are
from of old, from ancient times."
Micah 5:2 (NIV)

Mary and Elizabeth grew close during the time they spent together. Mary stayed with Elizabeth for about three months before she returned home. Elizabeth most certainly offered comfort to Mary, gave her strength, and affirmed her. She learned much from Elizabeth during this time; however, Joseph longed for Mary to come back to Nazareth.

Joseph quietly awaited her return. He trusted in the faithfulness of the Lord as he prayed to Him. He imagined the life he would have with his precious wife, and he focused his hands, head, and heart on the work of preparing for their life together. He used the tools of carpentry to turn blocks of wood into bowls and plates; rough-hewn planks of wood into smooth sanded tabletops and chairs; and smooth, sanded wood into a carved trunk for Mary to hold the few valuables that she had. As he worked, he would have prayed often for Mary's safe return and for her joy.

He would have imagined their life together as he worked with wood like juniper, oak, and olive that he had seasoned for use. Their furnishings and home would have been simple and modest, for they were poor. But they were wealthy in love, for God would surely bring His own Son into a home filled with love.

While Joseph was preparing for the life he was going to have with Mary, he was also preparing to care for and protect the miracle that grew in Mary's womb. Joseph would become the earthly father to the Son of God, the long-awaited Messiah. What awesome reverence and fear, humility and courage Joseph must have had!

So after 400 years of silence when the fullness of time had come, God was moving, and everything was changing!

After Mary returned to Nazareth, the joyous couple began their life together, daily offering their hearts to their great and loving God, and to each other. As they were establishing their home and creating a new life together, they were also preparing for the birth of Jesus.

There was an Old Testament prophecy that would be fulfilled that Mary and Joseph may or may not have known. Jesus would not be born in Nazareth. Jesus was to be born in a town ninety miles away from Nazareth—a little town called Bethlehem:

> *But you, Bethlehem Ephrathah, though you are small among the clans of Judah,*
> *out of you will come for me one who will be ruler over Israel, whose origins are*
> *from of old, from ancient times.*
> Micah 5:2 (NIV)

The book of Luke tells us that Caesar Augustus issued a decree that a census needed to be taken of the entire Roman world. All were required to go to their ancestral town to register. Because Joseph was from the line of David, it was necessary for him to travel to the Judean city of Bethlehem, the city of David. Mary was determined to join Joseph on this journey though she was great with child.

They travelled for miles and days. Mary rode on the back of a donkey while Joseph walked beside her. The journey was not easy. The nights were cold; the ground was hard; and the travel difficult. But they had hope, trust, and the Lord to lead them, and give them strength.

After long days of travel, they arrived at the walled city of Bethlehem. The small town was flooded with travelers who had returned to be registered for the census.

Joseph sought a place for them to stay. They needed a safe place to stay for it was likely that Jesus would be born while they were there. While young Mary would have loved to have the strong presence of her mother, she trusted that God who had chosen her to carry His son would indeed bring Him safely into this world.

Joseph longed to provide Mary with a place of comfort and safety. But with so many travelers in Bethlehem, there was no room for them. The journey had exhausted Mary, whose burden was heavy. Joseph felt sad that he wasn't able to secure a room for Mary to rest her tired and weary body.

They finally settled in a stable where animals were kept. They took their cloaks and blankets and spread them on the hay to form a bed. That night they found comfort in the stars that shone around them and the animals nearby that gave them warmth and comfort with their quiet, familiar sounds.

While they were staying in Bethlehem, the number of days were completed for Mary, and the babe was ready to be born! The time had come! The Savior of the world was about to be born to two chosen people who would struggle in hope and trust to bring Jesus, the Messiah, into the world.

Dear God, oh, how You always provide for Your people! I'm thankful for Mary and Joseph and the long journey they took to Bethlehem.

Additional Bible Reading
Luke 2:1-5

Ornament
Mary & Joseph, Donkey, Bethlehem, or Star

Extending the Day's Focus
The prophet Micah prophesied that Jesus would be born in Bethlehem, the City of David. So the God of the universe would bring about monumental events that would require Joseph to leave Nazareth and travel to Bethlehem. Only God could orchestrate events of such magnitude that the whole of the Roman Empire would be affected. When the Roman Emperor, Caesar Augustus, sent out the imperial command for all citizens of the Roman Empire to return to their ancestral homes to be registered, he had no idea that he was aiding in the fulfillment of Micah's Old Testament prophecy. God was working during the 400 years of silence to bring everything into place for the birth of His Son. Search the internet for the extent of the Roman Empire when this edict was given. How many people would this command have affected? In all of this massive empire, God was moving mountains to prepare the way for the birth of His Son. Journal or discuss your findings and thoughts.

There are many Christmas songs about the town of Bethlehem. The most popular is "O Little Town of Bethlehem." Listen to this beautiful song and read the lyrics. Who wrote this beautiful carol? What is your favorite verse? Share or journal your findings and thoughts.

Bethlehem means "house of bread." In Hebrew, Bethlehem is two words. *Beth* meaning 'house" and *lehem* meaning "bread." Jesus referred to Himself as the "Bread of Life." How fitting that Jesus was born in Bethlehem. Locate scriptures in the Bible where Jesus is referred to as the "Bread of Life." Journal or discuss your findings.

Whether it's warm muffins and coffee with a friend or toast and jam with your siblings after school, bread brings people together. Consider baking a loaf of bread to take to someone who is elderly, sick, or shut in. Give someone the gift of bread.

Bread is a common food, eaten at most meals; it satisfies our hunger and strengthens our physical bodies. Jesus, the "Bread of Life," satisfies our spiritual bodies with acceptance, forgiveness, love, grace, strength, and so much more. I can eat bread, but it won't satisfy another person's physical hunger. And I can receive Jesus and the gifts He offers, but it won't satisfy another person's need for Jesus. We all need our own relationship with Jesus; we must seek Jesus, the "Bread of Life." Discuss or journal about your need of Jesus. Do you depend on Jesus who is the "Bread of Life" for your daily strength? Let me encourage you to draw near to Jesus and reach out to Him every day.

December 24
Jesus the Messiah is Born; the Day Had Come!

A shoot will come up from the stump of Jesse; from his roots a Branch will bear fruit. The Spirit of the LORD will rest on him—the Spirit of wisdom and of understanding, the Spirit of counsel and of might, the Spirit of the knowledge and fear of the Lord—and he will delight in the fear of the LORD.
Isaiah 11:1-3 (NIV)

For to us a child is born, to us a son is given, and the government will be on his shoulders. And he will be called Wonderful Counselor, Mighty God, Everlasting Father, Prince of Peace. Of the greatness of his government and peace there will be no end. He will reign on David's throne and over his kingdom, establishing and upholding it with justice and righteousness from that time on and forever. The zeal of the LORD Almighty will accomplish this.
Isaiah 9:6-7 (NIV)

Mary and Joseph settled into the stable where animals were sheltered. They could feel the cold of the night because the stable was open to the weather, but they received warmth from the animals nearby; and warmth from their blankets and cloaks; and warmth from each other.

When the time came for Jesus, the King of Kings, to be born, Mary and Joseph looked at each other. Neither had foreseen that the Son of God would come into the world like this. Jesus, the Messiah, would be born in a stable! He only had a manger for His bed and meager supplies to keep Him safe and warm. They were far from their families' help and comfort.

The Lord had planned this moment for centuries, equipping many people who had served Him for this holy, holy moment. Mary and Joseph trusted the One True God who had guided them. They never forgot the angel's words. They loved and trusted each other. They believed that the God of the universe knew who they were and where they were. He had planned for this moment for hundreds and hundreds of years. The Savior who had been spoken of since the Garden of Eden was to be born in Bethlehem, the city of David. The One the people had hoped for and prayed about for hundreds and hundreds of years was coming.

When the fullness of time had come, Mary, with noble Joseph by her side, gave birth to Jesus, the long-awaited Messiah! Hallelujah! Glory to God in the highest! God had victoriously and triumphantly come to earth to be with His people! God had come in the form of a newborn babe. Immanuel, "God with us" was here in the flesh! The Old Testament prophecies were fulfilled. It was indeed a holy night!

> While they were there, the time came for the baby to be born, and she gave birth
> to her firstborn, a son. She wrapped him in cloths and placed him in a manger,
> because there was no guest room available for them.
> Luke 2:6-7 (NIV)

The Savior of the world had been born, but how would anyone know about His birth? Wouldn't God want to let the world know that His one and only Son had been born? How would anyone find out? And who would believe the truth that He had come to liberate us from sin and shame, despair and destruction, giving us life and "it to the full"? (John 10:10).

God had His own God-sized celebration planned! In the same way that God had planned for Jesus to come into the world, God had a plan for how Jesus would be known to the world:

> And there were shepherds living out in the fields nearby, keeping watch over their
> flocks at night. An angel of the Lord appeared to them, and the glory of the Lord
> shone around them, and they were terrified. But the angel said to them, 'Do not be
> afraid. I bring you good news that will cause great joy for all the people. Today in
> the town of David a Savior has been born to you; he is the Messiah, the Lord. This
> will be a sign to you: You will find a baby wrapped in cloths and lying in a manger.'
> Suddenly a great company of the heavenly host appeared with the angel, praising
> God and saying, 'Glory to God in the highest heaven, and on earth peace to those
> on whom his favor rests.' When the angels had left them and gone into heaven,
> the shepherds said to one another, 'Let's go to Bethlehem and see this thing that
> has happened, which the Lord has told us about.'
> Luke 2:8-15 (NIV)

How beautiful and how God-like for Him to announce Jesus' birth to lowly shepherds in nearby fields. God announced the birth of His extraordinary Son to ordinary people. He sent an angel to announce the birth of Jesus followed by a heavenly host of angels. They were all praising God!

God did not announce Jesus' miraculous birth to rulers or wealthy landowners or powerful politicians. God sent the announcement of His Son's birth to the humble and powerless, to the ordinary. God told the shepherds where to find baby Jesus. His announcement went to the ordinary who had no gifts to offer Jesus except their desire of heart and willingness to believe (John 6:29).

The shepherds' hearts jumped at the angels' words. "So they hurried off and found Mary and Joseph, and the baby, who was lying in the manger" (Luke 2:16). They could not contain their joy after visiting baby Jesus, Mary, and Joseph!

> *When they had seen him, they spread the word concerning what had been told them about this child, and all who heard it were amazed at what the shepherds said to them. But Mary treasured up all these things and pondered them in her heart. The shepherds returned, glorifying and praising God for all the things they had heard and seen, which were just as they had been told.*
> Luke 2:17-20 (NIV)

After Jesus was born, Magi, or Wise Men, came from the east to worship Him. They had been watching for years for the star that would signal the birth of the Messiah. When they came to Jerusalem, they asked, "Where is the one who has been born king of the Jews? We saw his star when it rose and have come to worship him" (Matthew 2:2).

They followed the light of the star "until it stopped over the place where the child was.... they saw the child with his mother Mary, and they bowed down and worshipped him. Then they opened their treasures and presented him with gifts of gold, frankincense, and myrrh" (Matthew 2:9-11). These were not ordinary gifts; they were highly prized, expensive gifts befitting a king. Offering these valuable gifts to baby Jesus showed they certainly did consider Him the King. The Magi surely knew that this child would one day be their Deliverer. And even more, He would be the ruler of all nations. After they worshipped Jesus and gave Him their gifts, they returned to the land they had come from.

Jesus' miraculous birth fulfilled the prophecy of Isaiah: "... the Lord himself will give you a sign: The virgin will conceive and give birth to a son and will call him Immanuel" (Isaiah 7:14). "Immanuel," means "God with us." Indeed, God, in the form of a baby, had come to earth to live among His people. To know that God is with you is the greatest, most miraculous, most life changing, most glorious gift we could ever receive!

God's plan to redeem His people came in the form of a baby born in a stable. Jesus came to redeem everyone from the lowly shepherds to the wealthy Wise Men. He came for me. He came for you!

O Holy Night
(By Placide Cappeau)
O holy night, the stars are brightly shining,
It is the night of our dear Savior's birth!
Long lay the world in sin and error pining,
'Till he appeared and the soul felt its worth.
A thrill of hope, the weary world rejoices,
For yonder breaks a new and glorious morn!
Fall on your knees!
Oh hear the angel voices!
Oh night divine.

Dear God, I am forever thankful for the miraculous birth of Jesus, the King of Kings, the One who brings salvation!

Additional Bible Reading
Matthew 2:1-12 and Luke 2:1-20

Ornament
Baby Jesus, Manger, Stable, Shepherds, Sheep, Wise Men, Gifts or Star

Extending the Day's Focus
Jesus was not born in Jerusalem or Rome or some other city of importance. He was born in Bethlehem, a small town of common people, where humans first laid their eyes on Immanuel, God in the flesh. Lowly shepherds announced His birth. A simple manger was His bed. A humble stable was His home. Jesus came for all of us! Discuss or journal what it means to you that Jesus came for everyone!

It's likely that the shepherds who came to worship Jesus were tending sheep that were being raised for temple sacrifices; they were shepherding sacrificial lambs. In this case, God announced to the shepherds the miraculous birth of the last sacrificial lamb, the Lamb of God. In John 1:29, John the Baptist refers to Jesus as, "the Lamb of God, who takes away the sin of the world!" Discuss or journal about the significance of God's announcement being made to lowly shepherds.

Jesus was visited by Magi. Do some research to find out more about them. How many would there have been? Where do scholars think they came from? How did they know to be looking for the star? Journal or discuss your findings.

The Magi brought gifts to baby Jesus. They brought gold, myrrh, and frankincense. What is myrrh? What was it used for? What is frankincense? What was it used for? What is the significance of these three items? Do you think other gifts were given to Jesus but not listed in the Bible? Discuss or journal your findings and thoughts.

Jesus' birth was the miraculous fulfilment of prophecy. The long-awaited Messiah was here! He had come to save all of us from our sin and give us life and life to the full ... just the way God made us to live. God gives us the freedom to choose a full life with Him through Jesus or a life of bondage through self-reliance. What are you choosing for your life? Journal your thoughts.

Read John 6:29. What does this verse mean to you? Journal or discuss your thoughts.

Conclusion

We all would hope that the birth of Jesus, Immanuel, would herald an immediate change in the hearts of all people. But it did not. There was an abundance of people who did not want Jesus to succeed in bringing others to salvation through God's love. The power and presence of salvation still required that Jesus go from being a baby who was cared for by His mother to being the Messiah who would save His own mother and everyone else who would receive Him as their Lord and Savior!

Jesus would later tell those who would listen that He was "the way and the truth and the life. No one comes to the Father except through me" (John 14:6). He also said, "I have come that they may have life, and have it to the full" (John 10:10).

We pray that you will go far beyond the birth of Jesus and learn more about His life, His sacrifice, His resurrection, and His return. We pray that you learn more about the love He came to share and the life He came to give us. He came to return us to be His image-bearers. He desires for us to become who He created us to be and do what He created us to do. God bless you.

The LORD bless you and keep you;
the LORD make his face shine on you and be gracious to you;
the LORD turn his face toward you and give you peace.
Numbers 6:24-26 (NIV)

About the Authors

Chip and Sonya Dodd were high school sweethearts. They have been married since 1983. Chip and Sonya live in Middle Tennessee and have two grown sons and two precious daughters-in-law. Sonya has two degrees in education, and Chip has a doctorate in counseling. Chip is a counselor, mentor, speaker, and writer. He is the author of several books, including *The Voice of the Heart* and *How Are You Feeling Today?*